NEW AGE

VOCABULARY

FOR ACHIEVERS

NEW AGE VOCABULARY FOR ACHIEVERS

(Useful for SAT, TOEFL, IELTS, GRE, GMAT etc.)

ANJANA AGARWAL

PUBLISHING FOR ONE WORLD

NEW AGE INTERNATIONAL (P) LIMITED, PUBLISHERS

New Delhi • Bangalore • Chennai • Cochin • Guwahati • Hyderabad

Jalandhar • Kolkata • Lucknow • Mumbai • Ranchi

Visit us at **www.newagepublishers.com**

Published by New Age International (P) Ltd., Publishers
First Edition: 2010

Branches:

- 36, Malikarjuna Temple Street, Opp. ICWA, Basavanagudi, **Bangalore**. ✆ (080) 26677815
- 26, Damodaran Street, T. Nagar, **Chennai**. ✆ (044) 24353401
- CE-39/1016, Carrier Station Road, Near Paulson Park Hotel, Ernakulam South, **Cochin.** ✆ (0484) 4051303
- Hemsen Complex, Mohd. Shah Road, Paltan Bazar, Near Starline Hotel, **Guwahati**. ✆ (0361) 2543669
- No. 105, 1st Floor, Madhiray Kaveri Tower, 3-2-19, Azam Jahi Road, Nimboliadda, **Hyderabad**. ✆ (040) 24652456
- RDB Chambers (Formerly Lotus Cinema) 106A,1st Floor, S.N. Banerjee Road, **Kolkata**. ✆ (033) 22275247
- 16-A, Jopling Road, **Lucknow**. ✆ (0522) 2209578
- 142C, Victor House, Ground Floor, N.M. Joshi Marg, Lower Parel, **Mumbai**. ✆ (022) 24927869
- 22, Golden House, Daryaganj, **New Delhi**. ✆ (011) 23262370, 23262368

ISBN : 978-81-224-2748-6

Rs. 295.00

C-09-06-3507

Printed in India at Glorious Printers, Delhi.
Typeset at Pagitek Graphics, Delhi.

PUBLISHING FOR ONE WORLD
NEW AGE INTERNATIONAL (P) LIMITED, PUBLISHERS
4835/24, Ansari Road, Daryaganj, New Delhi-110002
Visit us at **www.newagepublishers.com**

PREFACE

Need for good vocabulary

It is common knowledge that we need to communicate through language, through words. For us vocabulary is like a bank balance, we deposit in it from time to time through reading newspapers, magazines, books, watching television, and in conversation with other people and so on. We use this resource whenever we need it, during our communication, while studying, working or expressing ourselves in any situation. Our confidence, our clarity of ideas is expressed through our communication ability. Hence it is an essential requirement of our being successful and effective. **Being able to draw the right word at the right moment from our word bank is a very big asset in today's competitive world. Besides, several competitive exams also demand a strong lexical resource, be it SAT, TOEFL, IELTS, GRE, GMAT etc.** Thus, a strong word power makes a person confident about speaking in any situation, because he/she is never at a loss of words.

Need for the book

This book fulfils the need of students appearing for Engineering, MBA examinations, for corporate executives and for all those who wish to enhance their communication skills. Lot of research has gone into the designing of the format, layout and content of the book. Based on the extensive teaching and testing experience of the author, some high frequency words have been chosen keeping their relevance, usage, and need in mind.

USP of this book

There are several vocabulary books already in the market so why should somebody buy this book? **The answer to this question is this book's unique format, user-friendliness and usefulness**. Having handled students at different academic levels, having observed their competence or incompetence at communication, and having studied the efficacy of learning words in their context, has made the author reach this conclusion of putting words the way they are used, and what needs to be used when. That brings us to what the book contains.

Content of the book

Attempt has been made to first identify most frequently used words which pose a challenge to an average reader/user.

- **These words have been grouped together according to the category/theme which they belong to, so that their identification becomes easy.** Within this they have been put alphabetically so that if one needs to look up any word at any time, searching for it becomes very easy.
- **Each word is accompanied by its meaning and a sentence to exemplify its usage. A new concept of "my link" has been given to make the reader use the word in his/her own milieu**, so that it gets

related to his own experience and fixed in memory through that. In every chapter two such My link sentences have been made as examples.

- **Each chapter is then followed by a practice exercise, where the reader writes synonyms and antonyms of the words**. For some of the words you may feel that the synonyms are not actually synonyms rather their meaning or definition and the antonyms are not really opposites but clarifying what the word is not. This has been specifically done to make the user understand the word in simpler terms.
- Interactive exercises like Crosswords, Filling in the blanks, Matching the words etc., not only make remembering the word easier but also fun.
- Workbook pattern makes working in the book possible.

How to use the book

- Go in whichever order you feel comfortable.
- Focus on recalling words with minimum help, from outside sources.
- Keep testing/revising your newly learnt words so that they become a part of your active vocabulary.
- Take help from dictionary or thesaurus if you need more clarity on a certain word.
- Make more sentences of your own.
- Whenever you see a word which you have now learnt, in any reading context (say a newspaper or a book) concentrate on how it is being used. It will give you a very good feeling when you realise you know the word.

Anjana Agarwal

CONTENTS

Ch: 1 ADVENTURE & DARE — What's life without risk and chance!

ADVENTITIOUS happening by accident, casual (adj)

How it is used: Her **adventitious** arrival in the city of Berlin was quite historical as she got to witness the tearing down of the Berlin Wall.

My link: My meeting with my cousin at the New York airport was quite **adventitious**.

CALLOW youthful, immature (n)

How it is used: By making rude remarks about the college professors, he proved how **callow** he was.

My link: Even under peer influence, I can never speak about my teachers in such a **callow** manner, the way my classmates do.

CAPRICIOUS given to sudden change of mood or behaviour (adj)

How it is used: It was difficult to endure the strange whims and fancies of his **capricious** wife, but he bore all, ascribing it to her illness.

My link:

CAVALIER — showing lack of concern (adj)

How it is used: Strangely, a **cavalier** attitude in men, endears them to women, at least to start with.

My link:

CONTINGENCY — absence of certainty in events, a possibility (n)

How it is used: The new multi-storeyed hotel was questioned on its **contingency** evacuation plans in the wake of a disaster strike.

My link:

EFFRONTERY — insolence, impudence (n)

How it is used: Inspite of the fact that Dennis had never cared for his parents, he had the **effrontery** to ask them what they had done for him.

My link:

ENCOUNTER — unexpectedly meet, unpleasant struggle (n)

How it is used: Many dreaded criminals have been killed in **encounters** by dare-devil policemen.

My link:

ENTERPRISING showing initiative and boldness (adj)

How it is used: His **enterprising** nature made him successful even in new ventures across countries.

My link:

FORTUITOUS happening by chance (adj)

How it is used: Though the young couple claimed it otherwise, everybody suspected it was more of a coming together of two business houses than a mere **fortuitous** alliance of love.

My link:

GAMBOLLING running or jumping playfully (v)

How it is used: The **gambolling** deer was shot by the merciless hunters in one go.

My link:

HAZARDOUS dangerous, risky (adj)

How it is used: Handling inflammable material with carelessness can be extremely **hazardous**.

My link:

IMPETUOUS acting quickly and rashly (adj)

How it is used: Mary was **impetuous** enough to sell her house and its belongings, the moment she heard of her husband's foreign posting.

My link:

IMPRUDENT rash, not caring for consequences, lacking caution, injudicious (adj)

How it is used: It was **imprudent** of her to have spoken out of turn at the group discussion, and so she lost marks because of that.

My link:

INADVERTENT not achieved through deliberate planning (adj)

How it is used: There was an **inadvertent** delay in starting the play because one of the opening characters suddenly fainted backstage.

My link:

INDETERMINATE not exactly known, or defined (adj)

How it is used: Everybody felt that there had been an **indeterminate** increase in the prices of all household goods, though the government kept denying it.

My link:

INDISCRIMINATE done at random, without judgement (adj)

How it is used: Several civilians were caught in the **indiscriminate** firing at the disputed border area.

My link:

INTREPID fearless, adventurous (adj)

How it is used: The young captain belied his looks and turned out to be quite an **intrepid** person, steering the ship to safety.

My link:

JEOPARDIZE to put in a dangerous situation (v)

How it is used: There was no need for the bus driver to **jeopardize** everybody's life by indulging in a road race.

My link:

MAVERICK non-conformist, rebel (n)

How it is used: Being a **maverick** in the whole family of church-goers became more of a social-issue in the small village, than a religious one.

My link:

PRECARIOUS uncertain, not securely held (adj)

How it is used: It was a miracle how she clung to the rock in such a **precarious** manner, for two days, before the rescuers found her.

My link:

TEMERARIOUS reckless, rash (adj)

How it is used: Moving alone at night in an aimless manner, in what was considered as an unsafe area, was quite a **temerarious** step on the part of Sarah.

My link:

UNSCATHED unharmed, safe (adj)

How it is used: Many soldiers came back from the war, visibly **unscathed** and unharmed, but scarred from within.

My link:

VAGABOND someone who wanders about with no settled home (n)

How it is used: He neglected all his worldly duties, his business, his family and turned into a **vagabond**.

My link:

VOYAGE a long journey by sea or in space (n)

How it is used: Man's space **voyage** has always generated a lot of excitement and hype.

My link:

VULNERABLE exposed to being harmed (adj)

How it is used: Children are the most **vulnerable** to different kinds of air pollution caused by increasing traffic volumes in developing countries.

My link:

PRACTICE EXERCISE

Fill in the grid with the correct options in the blank spaces.

WORDS	SYNONYMS	ANTONYMS
1. vulnerable	exposed	____________
2. voyage	journey	N/A
3. vagabond	____________	home body
4. unscathed	____________	bring to harm
5. temerarious	____________	timid
6. precarious	____________	safe, certain
7. maverick	non-conformist	____________
8. jeopardize	____________	protect
9. intrepid	____________	fearful
10. indiscriminate	____________	careful
11. indeterminate	____________	fixed, certain
12. inadvertent	____________	intentional
13. imprudent	rash	____________
14. impetuous	hasty	____________
15. hazardous	dangerous	____________
16. gambolling	running around	N/A
17. fortuitous	____________	planned
18. enterprise	____________	lack initiative
19. encounter	meet	____________
20. effrontery	impertinence	____________
21. contingency	____________	certainty
22. cavalier	not caring	____________
23. capricious	____________	steadfast
24. callow	____________	mature
25. adventitious	casual	____________

N/A: Not applicable

REVIEW EXERCISE–1

Given below are words that you have learnt in this chapter. In front of each word are five options. Choose the option that most closely resembles the meaning of the word, and write the appropriate letter in the circles given. First one has been done for you.

Answer

1. cavalier

   (A) without concern (B) caring (C) shy (D) naughty (E) fearful — Answer: (A)

2. capricious

   (A) pathetic (B) mean (C) dramatic (D) whimsical (E) irregular — Answer: ( )

3. adventitious

   (A) adventurous (B) certainty (C) possibility (D) accidental (E) charming — Answer: ( )

4. contingency

   (A) emergency (B) possibility (C) group (D) disaster (E) condition — Answer: ( )

5. effrontery

   (A) to be in the front (B) insolence (C) hostility (D) courage (E) cursory — Answer: ( )

6. encounter

   (A) escape (B) meet (C) miracle (D) show unpleasantness (E) escape — Answer: ( )

7. hazard

   (A) danger (B) fear (C) sorrow (D) boredom (E) distance — Answer: ( )

8. imprudent

   (A) non-conformist (B) judgmental (C) injudicious (D) stubborn (E) wise — Answer: ( )

9. indeterminate
   (A) strong (B) undefined (C) precise
   (D) brazen (E) dogged
10. intrepid
   (A) timid (B) luke-warm (C) fearless
   (D) interior (E) interested
11. jeopardize
   (A) secure (B) dare-devilry (C) strike hard
   (D) ensure (E) endanger
12. maverick
   (A) conformist (B) obedient (C) daring
   (D) follower (E) rebel
13. unscathed
   (A) unsafe (B) exposed (C) scared
   (D) unfamiliar (E) unharmed
14. vulnerable
   (A) huggable (B) careful (C) brash
   (D) hasty (E) exposed
15. temerarious
   (A) adventurous (B) reckless (C) blatant
   (D) timorous (E) bashful

REVIEW EXERCISE–2

CROSSWORD

Given below is a crossword based on the words just learnt. With the help of the clues given fill in the right word.

Across

1. He roamed here and there like a ____________
2. A deer would do this in the forest ____________
3. A person who would start a new business will show ____________
4. A chance meeting would mean ____________
5. An immature, rash person would be called ____________

Down

1. Columbus went round the world on a ____________
2. If somebody had the cheek to reply his teachers back he would be showing ____________
3. If somebody is very moody, then he/she is ____________

Ch: 2

ART, DRAMA, MUSIC, CULTURE
—Finer aspects of life

ARTEFACT — object made by human-beings (n)

How it is used: The cultural richness of an ancient civilization is revealed by the discovery of different kinds of **artefacts** in the ruins.

My link: My house is full of traditional **artefacts** made very beautifully by my great grandmother.

BAROQUE — ornate and extravagant in style
ornate style of European architecture (adj)

How it is used: The costume ball was organised with attention to every little detail of baroque styling of the stage, dress and music.

My link: During my visit to London, I found several buildings in **baroque** architecture, looking even more majestic than the modern steel and glass towers.

CACOPHONY — a harsh mixture of sounds (n)

How it is used: In the old railway station building, millions of birds had made their nest resulting in a **cacophony** of sounds at both morning and evening time.

My link:

CADENCE rhythmic flow of words or sounds (n)

How it is used: It takes a fine ear to appreciate the **cadence** of nature like flowing of a stream or chirping of birds or humming of a bumble bee.

My link:

CRESCENDO increase in the volume in a piece of music, climax (n)

How it is used: Everybody marvelled at the way the soprano sang the delicate piece and handled the **crescendo** so effortlessly.

My link:

ECLECTIC deriving ideas from a broad range of resources (n)

How it is used: His style of writing was quite **eclectic**, drawing from various aspects of life.

My link:

IMPROVISE create or perform without preparation (v)

How it is used: Good actors are known to **improvise** as they go from dialogue to dialogue, and scene to scene.

My link:

LAMPOON publicly satirize or ridicule (n)

How it is used: In many countries one is not allowed to **lampoon** politicians or political leaders.

My link:

LINEAMENTS features especially of the face (n)

How it is used: The portrait artist was particularly good at sketching the **lineaments** of the clients' faces.

My link:

MEDLEY a varied mixture (n)

How it is used: Since the orchestra was put together in a hurry, the music it produced sounded more like a **medley** than a harmony.

My link:

MELLIFLUOUS musical and pleasing (adj)

How it is used: The **mellifluous** notes of the Solitary Reaper's song captivated Wordsworth's attention.

My link:

MIMICRY imitation of someone or something for entertainment purpose (n)

How it is used: He carved a flourishing career on TV out of **mimicry** of the famous political leaders.

My link:

MOSAIC a colourful pattern made by pieces of marble, tile or glass (n)

How it is used: The drifting sunlight through the stained glass windows made a **mosaic** on the polished marble floor of the church.

My link:

MURAL painting done directly on wall (n)

How it is used: The **murals** in the art museum were admired for their artistic charm and originality.

My link:

PANTOMIME acting without dialogues (n)

How it is used: The **pantomime** of the Nativity Scene by kindergarten students enthralled everybody.

My link:

PASTICHE imitation of another's style of art, music or writing (n)

How it is used: Today, what new generation singers call inspiration, is just a **pastiche** of old musicians' works.

My link:

PERCUSSION striking one solid object against another (n)

How it is used: **Percussion** instruments like drums were used by the tribes of Africa for sending signals to each other.

My link:

POT-POURRI a varied mixture, a medley (n)

How it is used: On first view, the shop looked like a **pot-pourri**, but had all kinds of knick-knacks to please every taste.

My link:

PROLOGUE an introduction to a play or poem (n)

How it is used: The **prologue** made it clear that the play was a modern day spoof on the story of the famous Shakespearian play – Midsummer Nights' Dream.

My link:

PROTEAN — able to adapt, versatile (adj)

How it is used: Very few actors have such a **protean** personality as Dustin Hoffman.

My link:

RACONTEUR — a skilful story teller (n)

How it is used: My grandfather is an excellent **raconteur** and entertains everybody with stories of his life.

My link:

REPERTOIRE — a collection or list of works of music, drama etc. (n)

How it is used: Every gifted musician has a **repertoire** of compositions ready for any occasion.

My link:

STACCATO — short abrupt sounds (n)

How it is used: The heavy-metal band sounded more like **staccato** noise than music.

My link:

THESPIAN — related to drama and theatre (n)

How it is used: Actors like Lawrence Olivier, Clint Eastwood are cut out for a **thespian** career.

My link:

TITILLATE — arouse to mild excitement (v)

How it is used: It is easy to **titillate** the audience, but to truly entertain them requires real talent.

My link:

TUTELAGE — guardianship, authority over someone (n)

How it is used: Under the **tutelage** of the master craftsman, the apprentice gained a lot of skill and sophistication.

My link:

UNISON — complete harmony (n)

How it is used: The church choir not only sang in **unison** but also in a melodious way.

My link:

VERSATILE — having many talents (adj)

How it is used: Very few children are as **versatile** as Joanna, she can dance, she can paint, she can act, she can sing as well.

My link:

VIGNETTE — brief description or account (n)

How it is used: The introduction to the book by the new author was accompanied by interesting **vignettes** of her life.

My link:

VIRTUOSO — a person highly skilled in music or arts (n)

How it is used: M.F. Husain is a real **virtuoso** artist renowned not only in India but internationally as well.

My link:

VISAGE — face, appearance, features (n)

How it is used: The cheerful **visage** of the princess indicated her warmth and popularity among the masses.

My link:

WARBLE to sing with trills and vibrations (n)

How it is used: She could hear the bird **warble** in the trees near her house, but could never see it.

My link:

PRACTICE EXERCISE

Match each word with its definition

Column A	Column B
1. warble	(a) harsh unpleasant sounds
2. visage	(b) skilful story teller
3. virtuoso	(c) collection of works of music, drama etc.
4. vignette	(d) a person highly skilled in music or arts
5. versatile	(e) a varied mixture
6. unison	(f) versatile, able to adapt
7. tutelage	(g) short abrupt sounds
8. titillate	(h) musical and pleasing
9. thespian	(i) features (especially of face)
10. staccato	(j) guardianship
11. repertoire	(k) colourful pattern made by marble, glass etc.
12. raconteur	(l) ornate style
13. protean	(m) related to drama, theatre
14. prologue	(n) made by hand
15. pot-pourri	(o) acting without dialogues
16. percussion	(p) striking of drums
17. pastiche	(q) painting done directly on wall
18. pantomime	(r) having many talents
19. mural	(s) imitation for entertainment
20. mosaic	(t) heterogenous mixture, medley
21. mimicry	(u) publicly satirize or ridicule
22. mellifluous	(v) deriving ideas from everywhere

Column A	Column B
23. medley	(w) brief description or account
24. lineaments	(x) imitation of other's style
25. lampoon	(y) arouse to mild excitement, tickle
26. improvise	(z) appearance, face
27. eclectic	(a^1) create or perform without preparation
28. crescendo	(b^1) rhythmic
29. cadence	(c^1) highest note
30. cacophony	(d^1) introduction to a play
31. baroque	(e^1) sing with vibrations
32. artefact	(f^1) complete harmony

REVIEW EXERCISE–1

Given below are words that you have learnt in this chapter. In front of each word are five options. Choose the option that is nearly opposite in meaning to the word and write the appropriate letter in the circles given. First one has been done for you.

Answer

1. improvise
   (A) rehearsed (B) make better (C) prove right (D) prompted (E) appropriate — Answer: (A)
2. lampoon
   (A) generosity (B) ridicule (C) glorify (D) weakness (E) cartoon — Answer: ( )
3. medley
   (A) unique (B) confusion (C) mixture (D) exclusive — Answer: ( )
4. eclectic
   (A) impressive (B) crazy (C) ancient (D) restricted (E) imaginative — Answer: ( )
5. versatile
   (A) multi-faceted (B) limited (C) enthusiastic (D) lively (E) wordy — Answer: ( )
6. mimicry
   (A) foolery (B) innovation (C) originality (D) mockery (E) copying someone — Answer: ( )
7. staccato
   (A) broken (B) abrupt (C) unpleasant (D) rhythmic (E) musical — Answer: ( )
8. crescendo
   (A) pitch (B) bass (C) noisy (D) high point (E) waterfall — Answer: ( )

9. prologue

(A) epilogue (B) after thought (C) introduction
(D) prelude (E) conclusion

10. cadence

(A) rhythm (B) disharmony (C) waves
(D) flow (E) coming down

11. tutelage

(A) mastery (B) authority (C) disciple
(D) coverage (E) slavery

12. mellifluous

(A) unpleasant (B) musical (C) lilting
(D) hard (E) malleable

13. protean

(A) versatile (B) vast (C) nutritious
(D) limited (E) artistic

14. virtuoso

(A) crude (B) skilled (C) talented
(D) amateur (E) truthful

15. pastiche

(A) original (B) mish-mash (C) pastry
(D) fetish (E) combination

16. titillate

(A) entertain (B) tickle (C) bore
(D) sober (E) excite

17. unison

(A) discord (B) harmony (C) unity
(D) permission (E) accord

18. cacophony

(A) noise (B) symphony (C) cactus
(D) harmony (E) telephonic

REVIEW EXERCISE–2

Now let's see if you are able to recall the words you have learnt in this chapter. A brief definition and the first letter have been given for your help. First one has been done for you.

1. features of the face — Lineaments
2. painting done on the wall — M ______________
3. acting without dialogues — P ______________
4. a story-teller — R ______________
5. a mixture — P ______________
6. short abrupt sounds — S ______________
7. a list of works of music, art etc. — R ______________
8. related to drama, cinema — T ______________
9. authority over someone — T ______________
10. appearance — V ______________
11. a brief account — V ______________
12. in harmony — U ______________
13. an introduction — P ______________
14. a kind of instruments — P ______________
15. man-made objects of artistic value — A ______________
16. singing of birds — W ______________
17. copying someone — M ______________
18. high note or climax — C ______________
19. colourful pattern of tiles — M ______________

Ch: 3 BEAUTY
—It lies in the eyes of the beholder

AESTHETIC — of pleasing appearance, concerned with beauty (adj)

How it is used: Her **aesthetic** sense of dressing up quite made up for her ordinary looks.

My link: My new house has been very aesthetically done up by my parents.

COMELY — agreeable (adj)

How it is used: Since the day he got married, his **comely** wife became everyone's favourite in the village.

My link: As against expectation, my new boss was comely and unassuming.

DIAPHANOUS — light, delicate (adj)

How it is used: Through the **diaphanous** curtains, the happenings inside the house could be easily seen.

My link:

EMBELLISH — to add extra detail and decorate (v)

How it is used: Some designers are known for **embellishing** their clothes with a lot of sequins and lace.

My link:

ETHEREAL — light, heavenly, delicate (adj)

How it is used: In order to depict the fairy in the new movie the director was looking for a thin, petite, ethereal beauty who could play the part well.

My link:

FILLIGREE — delicate ornamental work (adj)

How it is used: The **filligree** work on the marble lattices in the mausoleum was worth admiring.

My link:

FLAWLESS — perfect, blemish free (adj)

How it is used: Everybody thought that she had a **flawless** peaches and cream complexion.

My link:

FLORID flowery, intricate, elaborate (adj)

How it is used: Everybody in the audience agreed that the scholar's speech was definitely **florid**, though the essence was not too clear.

My link:

GOSSAMER very fine, spider-web like material (n)

How it is used: The children looked so pretty in their fairy costumes and **gossamer** wings, that the dance-drama was sure to be a grand success.

My link:

IDYLLIC blissful and peaceful (adj)

How it is used: A luxurious holiday in an **idyllic** spa is everybody's dream nowadays.

My link:

IMMACULATE perfectly clean, free from flaw (adj)

How it is used: Each student was given a brief to turn out in the most **immaculate** uniform for the passing out parade.

My link:

ORNATE highly, elaborately decorated (adj)

How it is used: The house was decorated with a lot of antique and **ornate** furniture.

My link:

PANACHE confidence of style, flair, flamboyance (adj)

How it is used: The new designer was confident about his out of the box designs and had a lot of **panache** about him.

My link:

PICTURESQUE visually attractive, charming (adj)

How it is used: The **picturesque** beauty of Switzerland bowled the tourists over.

My link:

PRISTINE unspoiled, in pure original condition (adj)

How it is used: The **pristine** surroundings of the beach resort were soothing enough to calm the most tired souls.

My link:

PULCHRITUDE beauty (n)

How it is used: The standards of female **pulchritude** keep changing from generation to generation.

My link:

SCINTILLATING sparkling, shining brightly (adj)

How it is used: The **scintillating** skyline of Dubai speaks for its architectural marvel in the desert.

My link:

URBANE refined, elegant (adj)

How it is used: Not only was Mr. Nicholson **urbane** and pleasing, his modesty defied his lineage.

My link:

VENEER a thin decorative covering; an outward appearance (n)

How it is used: As soon as the actress realised she had not been chosen for the lead role, the **veneer** of her sweetness gave away and all hell broke loose.

My link:

WINSOME attractive, appealing (adj)

How it is used: Her **winsome** manners popularised her as an excellent hostess at all parties.

My link:

PRACTICE EXERCISE

Choose the word which fits in best in the given blank in each sentence.

pulchritude, comely, embellishments, diaphanous, winsome, florid, scintillating, idyllic, filligree, picturesque, flawless, pristine, aesthetic, ornate, gossamer, immaculate, veneer, urbane

1. Indian dresses are not so strong on cuts and designs as they are on _______________ and detailing.
2. It was strange, how the twin sisters were opposite, while one was quiet and __________, the other was tomboyish and extrovert.
3. The _______________ gown with a taffeta lining was a brilliant idea for a wedding dress.
4. The silver ______________ necklace was so delicate and pretty that it caught everybody's attention.
5. His work was so _______________ that examiners did not know where to deduct marks.
6. It is difficult to believe how male designers have such an ______________ sense while most men don't have any.
7. It must be difficult to choose the winner at beauty pageants from among the several examples of female ______________.
8. His style of writing was unnnecessarily verbose and ______________.
9. Though the ______________ of the chairs was gone, yet it revealed expensive mahogany wood beneath.
10. The scenery of the Scottish countryside was _____________ and breathtaking.
11. Sometimes a ____________ personality makes up for ordinary looks.
12. If this craze for ____________ locations for exotic holidays continues, how many places will remain that way.
13. His description of the place was so_____________ that we could almost see his cottage and the hills around it.
14. The __________ performance the rising singer gave, made it evident that a new star was born.
15. The muslin of Dhaka used to be as fine as ____________ and attracted several British traders to the uniqueness of the material.
16. The interiors of the mansion were done up with the finest tapestry and most _________ of furniture.
17. The house was small but kept in such an _________ manner that it was really praise-worthy.
18. The guest lecturer's ___________ charm and knowledge of the subject impressed the students a lot.

REVIEW EXERCISE–1

CROSSWORD

Given below is a crossword based on the words just learnt. On the basis of the clues given, fill in the right word.

Across

1. If a scenery is very beautiful it would be _______________ .
2. If someone had a pleasing personality, one would be called _______________ .
3. If a situation is perfect it would be called _______________ .
4. A near perfect complexion is _______________ .
5. Having a sense of beauty is having _______________ sense.
6. Something which is very intricate is _______________ .
7. Fine web like material is _______________ .

Down

1. a material which is almost transparent is _______________
2. an agreeable person is _______________
3. to decorate is to _______________
4. delicate fine work is _______________

REVIEW EXERCISE–2

Now let us see if you are able to recognise the words you have learnt in this chapter. A brief definition and the first letter have been given for your help. First one has been done for you.

1. highly decorated — Ornate ____________
2. to add detail, or ornamental features — E ____________
3. delicate, fine work — F ____________
4. agreeable, pleasant — C ____________
5. perfect — I ____________
6. shining brightly — S ____________
7. spider-web thin — G ____________
8. pure, unspoiled — P ____________
9. flowery — F ____________
10. blissful, perfect — I ____________
11. a thin decorative covering — V ____________
12. attractive — W ____________
13. visually appealing — P ____________
14. related to beauty — A ____________
15. without a stain or scar — F ____________
16. beauty — P ____________
17. light, delicate — D ____________
18. sophisticated and genteel — U ____________
19. airy, light and heavenly — E ____________
20. flamboyance, style — P ____________

Ch: 4

COMMUNICATION —Make yourself heard

ACERBIC harsh, sharp in tone, sour in taste, as an unripe fruit (adj)

How it is used: Everybody in the group shunned her because she always had an **acerbic** comment to make.

My link:

No one in the family likes my aunt because of her **acerbic** tongue.

ARTICULATE fluent and clear in speech (adj)

How it is used: It was admirable how **articulate** the little boy was at that young age and how beautifully he spoke at the orientation programme.

My link:

My interview went very well because I was **articulate** and confident.

COGENT convincing, powerful, persuasive (adj)

How it is used: The jury could not overlook the defendant's pleas as his arguments were so **cogent** and earnest.

My link:

COHERENT — due agreement of ideas (adj)

How it is used: The candidate was so nervous at the interview that he had to be reminded again and again to be **coherent**.

My link:

COHESION — logical connection (n)

How it is used: Though the director had taken a very wide canvas for his film, but the **cohesion** of it was praiseworthy.

My link:

COLLOQUIAL — related to conversational or informal speech (adj)

How it is used: Modern literature has incorporated lot of changes in the languages and become more **colloquial**.

My link:

COMMUNIQUÈ — official announcement made to the media (n)

How it is used: The **communiquè** to the press about their marriage confirmed the rumours of their roaring affair.

My link:

DIALECTICAL relating to logical discussion of ideas and opinions (adj)

How it is used: All great statesmen have been known to possess great **dialectical** and oratorial skills.

My link:

DIATRIBE verbal attack, lengthy scolding (n)

How it is used: The opponents' **diatribe** against the ruling party was meant to embarrass and destabilise the government on the issue of price rise.

My link:

DIDACTIC containing principles or rules (adj)

How it is used: One can't win the teenagers over by being **didactic**, any advice has to be logical and given in a conversational manner.

My link:

DISCOURSE a talking together (n)

How it is used: The whole neighbourhood gathered for listening to the spiritual **discourse** of the zen master.

My link:

DISCURSIVE digressing from one subject to another (adj)

How it is used: Though the speech began well, it slowly turned into more and more **discursive** and veered away from the topic.

My link:

DIVULGE make known, reveal (v)

How it is used: It is not appropriate to **divulge** internal domestic matters to people from outside.

My link:

ELOQUENCE art of expressing in a clear manner (n)

How it is used: Betty's sharp **eloquence** and quickwittedness charmed everybody.

My link:

ENCOMIUM a speech or piece of writing expressing praise (n)

How it is used: The media showered **encomiums** on the performance put up by the little children.

My link:

ENUMERATE mention one by one (v)

How it is used: It's upto us if we want to **enumerate** people's faults or count their strengths.

My link:

ENUNCIATE say clearly and precisely (v)

How it is used: The board members asked the union leader to **enunciate** the union's demands in clear terms.

My link:

EXTEMPORIZE improvise, speak without preparation (v)

How it is used: Some leaders are born orators and can **extemporize** beautifully on any topic.

My link:

GARRULOUS talkative (adj)

How it is used: Amelia was considered to be so **garrulous** she could hold a guinness record in non-stop speaking.

My link:

GIBBERISH meaningless speech or writing (n)

How it is used: Lot of scientific predictions which were considered **gibberish** in nineteenth century have already become true.

My link:

GRANDILOQUENCE pompous or extravagant in language (n)

How it is used: After sometime the politician's **grandiloquence** stopped impressing the people, because they realised the emptiness of his words.

My link:

HARANGUE a forceful, aggressive speech (n)

How it is used: What had started as a inauguration speech of the new power plant soon turned into a **harangue** on the failures of the existing facility.

My link:

JARGON language used by particular profession or group (n)

How it is used: First we had medical **jargon**, then we had computer geeks talking in their new language, God knows what will be next.

My link:

LACONIC — using very few words (adj)

How it is used: Being laconic is a quality normally associated with men, imagine a woman being **laconic**.

My link:

LOQUACIOUS — given to continual talking (adj)

How it is used: It is a wonder how **loquacious** teenagers turn when they are on phone talking to their friends.

My link:

LUCID — clear, easily understood (adj)

How it is used: The presentation was on a very technical problem but was done in a clear and **lucid** manner.

My link:

ORATORY — art of formal public speaking (n)

How it is used: Samuel became a favourite candidate for the college elections from day one because of his excellent skills in **oratory**.

My link:

PARLANCE particular way of using words (n)

How it is used: If one goes deeply into the nuances of a language, one will realise that there are several phrases which are special to the local **parlance**.

My link:

PROLIXITY excessive wordiness (n)

How it is used: The **prolixity** of his speech became insufferable after some time.

My link:

RECANT renounce a former opinion or belief (v)

How it is used: When Galileo propounded his theories, the conformists wanted him to **recant** his statements.

My link:

REITERATE say something repeatedly (v)

How it is used: The landlady **reiterated** her demands for the pending rent, once she realised Jenny had got some money.

My link:

RETICENT — reserved, not revealing one's feelings (n)

How it is used: Since it was a high level case involving several senators and governors, the FBI was **reticent** in taking any names.

My link:

RHETORIC — impressive language but lacking sincerity (n)

How it is used: The workers knew that their leader's long lecture was just plain **rhetoric** because he was powerless to do anything much.

My link:

SOLILOQUY — talking to oneself (n)

How it is used: Since it was a modern interpretation, Hamlet's **soliloquies** were also set upon today's youth's problems.

My link:

TACIT — implied without being said (adj)

How it is used: It was revealed much later that every controversial deal had the mafia's **tacit** approval.

My link:

TACITURN reserved in speech, speaking little (adj)

How it is used: It wasn't difficult to understand how the grave tragedy of her husband's murder had made her so **taciturn**.

My link:

TIRADE long speech of angry criticism (n)

How it is used: The entire staff was expecting a long **tirade** from the boss for the heavy loss the company was accruing.

My link:

VALEDICTORY related to farewell (adj)

How it is used: The **valedictory** speech was really touching and moved everyone to tears.

My link:

VERNACULAR language spoken by ordinary people of a region (adj)

How it is used: Will the popularity of English make the usage of **vernacular** medium in countries like India unviable?

My link:

VERBATIM exactly same words as original (adv)

How it is used: The interview was telecast **verbatim** and created a furore on the world's political scene.

My link:

VITUPERATIVE abusive and bitter (adj)

How it is used: The **vituperative** atmosphere in the house because of the parents' constant fighting affected the emotional state of the children.

My link:

PRACTICE EXERCISE

Fill in the grid with the correct options in the blank spaces.

WORDS	SYNONYMS	ANTONYMS
1. vituperative	abusive	____________
2. vernacular	____________	literary
3. verbose	____________	concise
4. verbatim	word to word	____________
5. valedictory	farewell speech	____________
6. tirade		praise
7. taciturn	____________	talkative
8. tacit	implicit	____________
9. soliloquy	____________	dialogue
10. rhetoric	empty talk	____________
11. reticent	reserved	____________
12. reiterate	repeat	____________
13. recant	____________	re-assert
14. prolixity	verbosity	____________
15. parlance	____________	common language
16. oratory	____________	N/A
17. lucid	____________	confused
18. loquacious	____________	quiet
19. laconic	reticent	____________
20. jargon	parlance	____________
21. harangue	scolding	____________
22. gibberish	____________	sensible talk
23. garrulous	loquacious	____________
24. enunciate	propound	____________
25. enumerate	____________	N/A

WORDS	SYNONYMS	ANTONYMS
26. extemporize	__________	rehearse and speak
27. encomium	__________	criticism
28. eloquence	__________	confused talk
29. divulge	reveal	__________
30. discursive	digressing	__________
31. discourse	__________	N/A
32. didactic	moralistic	__________
33. diatribe	scolding	__________
34. dialectical	logical discussion	__________
35. communiquè	official announcement	__________
36. colloquial	spoken	__________
37. cohesion	__________	disjointed
38. coherent	logical	__________
39. cogent	convincing	__________
40. articulate	__________	incoherent
41. acerbic	__________	sweet

N/A: Not applicable

REVIEW EXERCISE–1

Choose the answer that most closely resembles the meaning of the word and fill in the option in the circle given. First one has been done for you.

Answer

1. didactic

(A) static (B) communicative (C) sweet talking (D) moralistic (E) clear — Answer: D

2. eloquence

(A) charming (B) talkative (C) reticence (D) pleasing (E) art of speaking clearly

3. vituperative

(A) violent (B) vindictive (C) talkative (D) abusive (E) sharp

4. soliloquy

(A) dialogue (B) oblique (C) lonely (D) solitude (E) monologue

5. loquacious

(A) talkative (B) well-mannered (C) polished (D) silent (E) lucrative

6. rhetoric

(A) long lecture (B) impressive (C) questioning (D) rules of speaking (E) insincere

7. encomium

(A) praise (B) principles (C) expression (D) decorum (E) many words

8. verbose

(A) descriptive (B) grammar (C) flowery (D) elaborate (E) having many verbs

9. acerbic

(A) vinegar (B) terrific (C) bitter

(D) acidic (E) unripe

10. cogent

(A) weak (B) powerful (C) true

(D) ineffective (E) coherent

11. communiquè

(A) press release (B) oblique comment (C) indirect

(D) communication (E) reserved

12. oratory

(A) public speaking (B) formality (C) loud

(D) oral (E) debating

13. reiterate

(A) repeat (B) reduce (C) remember

(D) remind (E) request

14. coherent

(A) logical (B) present (C) combination

(D) loose (E) inhabitant

15. cohesion

(A) joined together (B) tough (C) tight

(D) glued (E) comprehension

16. discourse

(A) argument (B) dialogue (C) advice

(D) discussion (E) lecture

17. diatribe

(A) digress (B) tribal (C) scolding

(D) bitterness (E) discussion

18. lucid

(A) clear (B) difficult (C) acidic

(D) transparent (E) fluid

19. recticent

(A) out spoken (B) reserved (C) powerful
(D) witty (E) sufficient

20. vernacular

(A) regional (B) spectacular (C) sophisticated
(D) literary language (E) ordinary language

21. divulge

(A) unknown (B) mystery (C) reveal
(D) convey (E) speak

22. tirade

(A) lecture (B) diatribe (C) briefing
(D) charade (E) tiresome

23. gibberish

(A) nonsense (B) gullible (C) grimace
(D) jabber (E) peevish

24. dialectical

(A) talking loudly (B) calm (C) local language
(D) diabolical (E) art of debate

25. jargon

(A) terminology (B) jovial (C) aggressive
(D) light-hearted conversation (E) chatter

26. laconic

(A) verbose (B) lambast (C) to the point
(D) wise (E) grief

27. recant

(A) repeat (B) disclaim (C) recount
(D) incantation (E) remember

28. parlance

(A) greeting (B) native (C) grammatical
(D) exaggeration (E) idiom

29. tacit

(A) spoken (B) neutral (C) understood

(D) written (E) abstract

30. taciturn

(A) turn of events (B) unspoken (C) unwritten

(D) tacit (E) talking little

31. enumerate

(A) enlist (B) describe (C) learned

(D) mention (E) numbers

32. enunciate

(A) expense (B) propound (C) murmur

(D) speak clearly (E) mumble

33. colloquial

(A) agreeable (B) literary (C) comprising

(D) conversational (E) discussion

34. harangue

(A) long speech (B) rancour (C) inspired

(D) harass (E) noisy

35. discursive

(A) joined handwriting (B) digressing (C) disjointed

(D) discussing (E) philosophical

REVIEW EXERCISE–2

There are two set of lists given. In list A fill in the words from within the chapter that mean the opposite to the words given. In list B fill in words from within the chapter which mean nearly the same as the words given.

List A	ANTONYMS
1. verbose	____________
2. tirade	____________
3. articulate	____________
4. garrulous	____________
5. gibberish	____________
6. loquacious	____________
7. recant	____________
8. divulge	____________

List B	SYNONYMS
1. vituperative	____________
2. vernacular	____________
3. parlance	____________
4. lucid	____________
5. taciturn	____________
6. verbosity	____________
7. grandiloquence	____________

Ch:5

DECEPTION OR LIE
—Speak truth or die

ABJURE — renounce a claim or oath (v)

How it is used: It was strange how easily Delilah **abjured** her views under pressure from the church.

My link: The military general of our nation was forced to **abjure** his views about cross-border terrorism by our politicians.

ADULTERATED — mixing inferior substance, corrupt (v)

How it is used: Several infants have been reported sick because of drinking milk which was found to be **adulterated** with melamine.

My link: One day it seemed to me that the juice I was having was **adulterated**.

AFFECTATION — pretension (n)

How it is used: Ever since she got a job at the royal household, her behaviour turned so **affectatious** as if she had herself turned into a queen.

My link:

APOCRYPHAL — considered, to be authentic but not true (adj)

How it is used: Though the people believe that the huge lake was formed by a meteorite falling at that place, but is not backed by scientific proof, and the tale appears to be largely **apocryphal**.

My link:

ARTIFICE — skilled trickery, clever deception (n)

How it is used: When Snow White could not be killed by other means, the queen tried to eliminate her through **artifice**.

My link:

BEGUILE — to deceive, cheat, mislead (v)

How it is used: The film producers **beguiled** the actor into investing his money in their next venture promising him of it being an assured hit.

My link:

BELIE — contradict, misrepresent (v)

How it is used: Her sweet words **belied** her venomous nature, and initially fooled people into believing her to be as innocent as she looked.

My link:

CHARADE — pretense (n)

How it is used: The whole exercise in elections was just a **charade** because the people were too scared to vote against the despot.

My link:

CHICANERY — use of trickery to achieve one's purpose (n)

How it is used: Knowing the murder case would not go in his client's favour the lawyer tried to use every bit of lie and **chicanery** to mislead the jury.

My link:

CIRCUMLOCUTION — long roundabout way of saying something (n)

How it is used: The employees couldn't believe that the company bosses had completely **circumlocuted** the main issue of increasing the salary, and had rather criticised their working.

My link:

COLLUSION — secret co-operation in order to cheat (n)

How it is used: It is difficult for the common people to understand how many economic decisions are taken because of the **collusion** of the powerful tobacco lobby or cosmetic giants.

My link:

CONNIVE conspire, to get together to do a wrong (v)

How it is used: Sometimes politicians **connive** with the bureaucracy and divert developmental funds towards their constituency.

My link:

CONTRABAND something which is forbidden by law, illegal trade (adj)

How it is used: The Border Task Force impounded several trucks carrying **contraband** goods at the border check post.

My link:

CREDULITY belief on slight evidence (n)

How it is used: Since she was new to the glamour world lot of people tried to take advantage of her **credulity**.

My link:

DELUSION a false belief (n)

How it is used: It was difficult for her to come out of her **delusion** and face the reality that her husband had actually died and would never come back.

My link:

DEVIOUS winding and dishonest (adj)

How it is used: The sequel to the superhero movie came with the villain shown to be even more **devious** and menacing than before.

My link:

FEIGN pretend (v)

How it is used: For centuries, children have **feigned** illness of some sort whenever they have not wanted to go to school.

My link:

DISSEMBLE disguise/hide one's feelings/pretend (v)

How it is used: Though he tried to **dissemble** his status, very soon the news of his being reduced to a pauper, spread in the town.

My link:

DUBIOUS not to be relied upon (adj)

How it is used: As his means of earning money become more **dubious**, people began to question his reputation.

My link:

EQUIVOCATION use of ambiguous language in order to deceive (n)

How it is used: The government thought that **equivocation** of the terrible crisis they were facing would, for some time, allay people's fear of a complete breakdown.

My link:

FABRICATE to make, to manufacture, to invent, with deceitful intent (v)

How it is used: The witness **fabricated** the whole account so skilfully that it appeared true.

My link:

FACADE front face (of a building), false appearance (n)

How it is used: People mistook their show of opulence to be real, no one realised it was a clever **facade** they had built up to hide their complete bankruptcy.

My link:

FACTITIOUS artificial, unnatural (adj)

How it is used: Celebrities are so used to living in a **factitious** world of fame and glamour, they can't relate to the ordinariness of the real world.

My link:

FALLACY a false idea or opinion (n)

How it is used: That Morton would improve in his wayward ways as he would grow up turned out to be a **fallacy**, he only grew worse.

My link:

FRAUDULENCE deception (n)

How it is used: The income that he had generated through **fraudulent** means could not become useful for any member of his family.

My link:

ILLICIT forbidden by law or custom (adj)

How it is used: Since the sting operation had used **illicit** means to trap the offender, the court refused to acknowledge the same as an evidence.

My link:

IMPOSTURE act of assuming false identity (n)

How it is used: His act of **imposture** as a foreign diplomat landed him in jail.

My link:

IMPROBITY wickedness, dishonesty (n)

How it is used: He had been their trusted servant for years, and it was difficult to believe that he was capable of this act of **improbity**.

My link:

INSINUATE suggest/hint in an indirect or unpleasant manner (v)

How it is used: The mafia leaders cleverly **insinuated** many youngsters to join their gang.

My link:

INVEIGLE persuade by deception (v)

How it is used: Half of the young men are **inveigled** into joining the terrorist groups by playing on their religious sentiments.

My link:

LARCENY theft (n)

How it is used: Since the act of the accused was most blatant and repeated he was charged with the more serious charge of **larceny** and not robbery.

My link:

MENDACITY untruthfulness (n)

How it is used: The habitual **mendacity** of Bob Brown left him with zero credibility in the area.

My link:

PERFIDIOUS deceitful, treacherous (adj)

How it is used: No one could believe that Macbeth who was considered most loyal to king Duncan, would commit such a **perfidious** act of murdering him.

My link:

PERJURY wilfully tell untruth in court under oath (n)

How it is used: To save his skin, the witness resorted to committing **perjury**, not realising the consequences of his action.

My link:

PREVARICATE speak or act evasively (v)

How it is used: Not knowing how to save himself on camera, the minister tried to **prevaricate** the whole issue of kickbacks.

My link:

SEMBLANCE outward appearance (n)

How it is used: Once the **semblance** of sophistication is over, out comes a crude person from within almost all of us.

My link:

SIMULATION put on the form of another (n)

How it is used: Artificial intelligence is **simulating** human intelligence to such an extent that it is feared the difference might cease to exist.

My link:

SLANDER false/malicious statement (n)

How it is used: What had initially caught the attention of the public, turned out to cheap **slander**, about their local hero.

My link:

SOPHISTRY clever but fallacious arguments (n)

How it is used: Most of the debate that goes around in the Parliament is a clever piece of **sophistry** meant to confound the public.

My link:

SPURIOUS false/fake (adj)

How it is used: **Spurious** drugs and medicines are becoming more and more difficult to detect.

My link:

STRATAGEM to outwit an opponent (n)

How it is used: Lot of crucial battles in history have been won on the bases of **strategem** and deceit.

My link:

PRACTICE EXERCISE

Fill in the grid with the correct options in the blank spaces.

WORDS	SYNONYMS	ANTONYMS
1. stratagem	deceptive plan, trickery	__________
2. spurious	__________	genuine
3. sophistry	fallacious arguments	__________
4. slander	libel, false statement to defame	__________
5. simulation	feign, put on an act	__________
6. semblance	outward appearance	__________
7. prevaricate	speak lie, evade truth	__________
8. perjury	false testimony under oath	__________
9. perfidious	__________	loyal
10. mendacity	__________	truthfulness
11. larceny	__________	N/A
12. inveigle	persuade by deception	__________
13. insinuate	imply	__________
14. improbity	__________	honesty
15. imposture	adopting a false identity	__________
16. illicit	__________	legal
17. fraudulence	deceit	__________
18. feign	pretend	__________
19. fallacy	__________	truth
20. factitious	__________	natural, not contrived
21. facade	false appearance	__________
22. fabricate	__________	give a true account
23. equivocation	misleading, concealing the truth	__________

WORDS	SYNONYMS	ANTONYMS
24. dubious	questionable	________
25. dissemble	________	speak straight
26. devious	dishonest, scheming	________
27. delusion	________	truth
28. credulity	easily convinced	________
29. contraband	smuggling, illegal trade	________
30. connive	plot, come together to do wrong	________
31. collusion	come together, conspire to cheat	________
32. circumlocution	________	direct, to the point
33. chicanery	deception	________
34. charade	pretense	________
35. belie	contradict	________
36. beguile	________	show correct path
37. artifice	deception	________
38. affectation	________	natural
39. adulterated	________	pure, original
40. abjure	vow	________

N/A: Not applicable

REVIEW EXERCISE–1

Given along with each sentence are three words. Choose the option which fits best in the given blank in the sentence.

1. Her face did not have even a ____________ of remorse at her husband's death.
   (semblance, prevarication, mendacity)
2. Though the whole town knew that he had become rich through ____________ means, yet no one had the courage to say it at the lavish parties he threw.
   (simulated, prevaricating, fraudulent)
3. Customs department confiscated a huge consignment of ____________ perfumes and watches of famous brands.
   (fabricated, spurious, illicit)
4. As success went to her head, Palomi began to have the ____________ that she was the most sought after model and could get away with any demands.
   (delusion, collusion, simulation)
5. Samuel entered the corporate world with the ____________ that money and good life could be had for asking.
   (chicanery, fallacy, turpitude)
6. People generally gave Mark a half an hour earlier time than needed because of his ____________ record of reaching on time.
   (dubious, beguiling, slanderous)
7. Committing ____________ is a serious offence.
   (perjury, artifice, sophistry)
8. Though Martha did not say so, but her words very clearly ____________ that she held Bob's parents responsible for their break-up.
   (simulated, adulterated, insinuated)
9. Detective Colin had worked hard to crack the case of ____________ in the town of Montgomery, and saw to it that the thief was charged for maximum punishment.
   (larceny, perjury, improbity)
10. In order to crack difficult criminal cases, a detective needs to have acumen to first understand the ____________ behind the case and then the crime itself.
    (stratagem, simulation, fallacy)
11. Whenever government has imposed restrictions on free import and export of certain goods, it has only encouraged ____________ trade in them.
    (contraband, spurious, illicit)
12. The Boston family had only heard about a prodigal uncle of theirs, and had never seen him, so they could never realise that the man was an ____________ and not their real uncle.
    (imposter, artifice, imposture)
13. Gloria was duped again and again because of her ____________, yet she trusted people blindly.
    (improbity, credulity, fallacy)

14. When Deborah was asked the whereabouts of her gym instructor she __________ complete ignorance.

(fabricated, insinuated, feigned)

15. Over the years Larsen had gathered a reputation of being capable of any kind of __________ to fund his drug addiction.

(credulity, improbity, adulteration)

16. In stories and fairy tales, step-mothers have been stereotypically shown as being __________ and mean.

(devious, dubious, spurious)

17. In professions like those of pilots, astronauts, __________ of real conditions is done so as to acclimatise the trainees.

(circumlocution, simulation, equivocation)

18. Coast Guard Force is forever trying to check entry of __________ goods like gold, drugs, fake items and animals etc.

(contraband, fabricated, simulated)

19. The government was baffled at the quantum of __________ that was taking place in everyday foods, milk products and confectionery items.

(affectation, adulteration, insinuation)

20. What a __________ it was when everybody was asked to gather at the reading of the will of Mr. Smith and the lawyer announced that everything had been given away to charity.

(facade, fabrication, charade)

REVIEW EXERCISE–2

(a) In list A are given some words. In list B are given words which mean more or less the same as in list A in a jumbled order. Match them to find words closest in meaning to each other.

List A	List B
1. fabricate	(a) collusion
2. connive	(b) belie
3. slander	(c) fraudulence
4. delusion	(d) prevarication
5. beguile	(e) facade
6. artifice	(f) fallacy
7. perfidious	(g) sophistry
8. semblance	(h) factitious
9. affectation	(i) vilify
10. equivocation	(j) chicanery
11. stratagem	(k) inveigle
12. mendacity	(l) dissemble

(b) To give more clarity on the words learnt in this chapter, let us do one more exercise. Below are given some definitions which are opposite to the given words. Out of the two options tick the appropriate one in the box given.

1. Trustworthy	–	dubious	☐
		devious	☐
2. Reality	–	collusion	☐
		delusion	☐
3. Speak truth	–	prevaricate	☐
		probity	☐
4. Logical argument	–	slander	☐
		sophistry	☐
5. Can never commit any treachery	–	perfidious	☐
		factitious	☐
6. Speak truth under oath	–	larceny	☐
		perjury	☐
7. Persuade somebody with honesty	–	inveigle	☐
		beguile	☐
8. Truthfulness	–	credulity	☐
		mendacity	☐
9. True, correct picture	–	fallacious	☐
		fraudulence	☐
10. Make pure	–	adulterate	☐
		insinuate	☐

Ch:6 DETERMINATION & STRENGTH, ENERGY & POWER

—You can do it if you want to

ARDOUR passion, zeal (n)

How it is used: Any movement needs a lot of **ardour** and involvement of committed people who believe in the cause.

My link:

I have decided to stick to my exercise routine with complete **ardour** and discipline.

ASSIDUOUS great care and perseverance (adj)

How it is used: The building of the Taj Mahal was the result of the **assiduous** labour of several thousands of artisans and masons.

My link:

My **assiduous** efforts at cracking the mathematics questions finally bore fruit.

BUTTRESS strengthen or support (v)

How it is used: Under siege from the plunderers, they **buttressed** the tribe's settlements with a high stone wall.

My link:

DAUNTLESS fearless and determined (adj)

How it is used: **Dauntless** knights in shining armour on fleet-footed horses are the stuff of many medieval romantic stories.

My link:

DILIGENT persistent (adj)

How it is used: **Diligent** efforts of the sales team saw a remarkable spurt in the sale of the company's products.

My link:

DOGGED persistent (adj)

How it is used: The thief could be caught only after a long, **dogged** chase by the police.

My link:

FORMIDABLE inspiring fear because of its strength and power (adj)

How it is used: The gap between the rich, and poor has always been **formidable** and has only made the poor people more frustrated.

My link:

FORTITUDE — courage in adversity (n)

How it is used: Sometimes circumstances make even common people show such **fortitude** that its amazing.

My link:

FRENETIC — wildly energetic (adj)

How it is used: Rock music has this inexplicable **frenetic** tempo which is hard to resist or not like.

My link:

FRENZY — mad excitement/wild behaviour (n)

How it is used: The carnival time in Brazil is a time of great **frenzy** and merry making.

My link:

IMPERMEABLE — not allowing anything (liquid) to pass through (adj)

How it is used: The new material was considered to be **impermeable** and was extensively recommended to be used for tents, hot-air balloons and even collapsible ceilings.

My link:

IMPETUS driving force, or energy (n)

How it is used: Environmental awareness & conservation needs more **impetus**, both monetary and ideological, from the developed countries.

My link:

IMPREGNABLE unable to be overcome, strong (adj)

How it is used: The king could save his and his subjects' lives because of the **impregnable** fort.

My link:

INDEFATIGABLE tireless (adj)

How it is used: Mountain climbing is as much an exercise in **indefatigable** endurance and energy as it is of careful planning.

My link:

INDOMITABLE impossible to subdue or defeat (adj)

How it is used: The British were quite perplexed at Gandhiji's **indomitable** spirit and non-violent methods.

My link:

INEXTRICABLE — impossible to escape from or separate (adj)

How it is used: The poachers had laid the trap so cruelly that the elephant injured itself and was still **inextricable**.

My link:

INVINCIBLE — too powerful to be defeated (adj)

How it is used: Every king, who has thought of himself as being **invincible**, has ultimately bitten dust.

My link:

JUGGERNAUT — huge overwhelming force (n)

How it is used: The Tsunami waves were a **juggernaut**, swallowing anything that came their way.

My link:

POTENCY — power, effect (n)

How it is used: Each homoeopathic drug comes with a specified dosage and **potency**.

My link:

PROWESS — skill or expertise in something, bravery in battle (n)

How it is used: The young prodigy showed great **prowess** and maturity in the game of chess.

My link:

REDOUBTABLE — causing fear, formidable (adj)

How it is used: The moment Sylvia realised how **redoubtable** the mafia lord was, she withdrew her complaint and decided to reach a compromise.

My link:

TENACIOUS — keeping a firm hold (adj)

How it is used: The opposition party's **tenacious** views against the nuclear deal led to the ultimate breakdown of talks between the countries.

My link:

TRENCHANT — forceful, vigorous (adj)

How it is used: The **trenchant** one man show of the comedian in the new play surpassed all his previous acts and broke all records.

My link:

VEHEMENT — showing strong feeling or vigour (adj)

How it is used: The Hippie movement was a **vehement** denial by a whole generation, of established norms and culture.

My link:

VIRILE — having manly strength, energy (adj)

How it is used: Lot of men think that being chauvinistic is similar to being **virile** and brave.

My link:

VITALITY — strong and active, energy (n)

How it is used: After extreme dry conditions, the rains brought a new freshness and **vitality** to the whole environment.

My link:

VIVACIOUS — lively and energetic (adj)

How it is used: The whole village was charmed by the **vivacious** bride of Mr. Smith, who went on to make friends with the village folk quite easily.

My link:

ZEALOUS having great energy or enthusiasm for a cause (adj)

How it is used: Putting everyone's opinions aside, the **zealous** film-maker went on to make the offbeat film and also win praises and success for it.

My link:

PRACTICE EXERCISE

Fill in the grid with the correct options in the blank spaces.

WORDS	SYNONYMS	ANTONYMS
1. zealous	______	unenthusiastic
2. vivacious	lively	______
3. vitality	vigour	______
4. virile	______	wimpy
5. vehement	______	mild
6. trenchant	forceful	______
7. tenacious	determined	______
8. prowess	______	cowardice
9. potency	______	powerless
10. inextricable	______	loose, untied
11. indomitable	unyielding	______
12. indefatigable	______	tired
13. impregnable	______	vulnerable
14. impetus	force, push	______
15. impermeable	impervious	______
16. frenzy	excitement	______
17. frenetic	frantic	______
18. fortitude	______	timidity
19. dogged	determined	______
20. diligent	persistent	______
21. dauntless	bold	______
22. assiduous	______	lazy
23. ardour	excitement	______

REVIEW EXERCISE–1

Choose the word which fits in best in the given blank in each sentence.

vitality, zealously, vivacious, impregnable, assiduous, ardour, vehement, frenzy, impermeable, trenchant, potent, diligence, fortitude, inextricably, impetus

1. He wooed Amelia with such __________ that she had no option but to say yes.
2. Sana's parents knew that her __________ would definitely show results one day.
3. The more Dorothy tried to get out of the complex situation, the more __________ she found herself trapped in it.
4. Sam had almost decided to change his job and was just waiting for one final __________.
5. When the townspeople realised that the municipal authorities were not going to remove the garbage due to the strike, they themselves got down to remove it with their __________ efforts.
6. The tired army was losing out in the long drawn battle till it got a __________ push by the reinforcements that began to arrive.
7. The new space-suits are light weight, collapsible, and made of thin __________ material.
8. Several children were selected from all over the country to be given awards for their __________ and courage.
9. In ancient times, city walls were supposed to be __________ and meant to protect the population from foreign invasions.
10. There was a lot of __________ and excitement at the Annual Mad Tea Party Festival held in the small hill town.
11. The severe drought had left the animals in the forest without any food, water and __________ .
12. John's rebellion against the family rules and regulations was a sign of his __________ nature.
13. Lot of young people take a break from regular corporate careers to __________ pursue their hobbies and vocations.
14. The __________ little children at the annual Spring Festival at the Spanish town were a sight to watch.
15. The destruction caused in the coastal town was a testimony to how __________ the storm must have been.

REVIEW EXERCISE–2

A. Below are given some words. Also given are four qualities under which they can be classified. Put the right quality against each.

(A) Courage (B) Power (C) Persistence (D) Strength (E) Excitement (F) Determination

(a) assiduous, diligent, dogged ____________

(b) impregnable, impermeable, indomitable, invincible ____________

(c) dauntless, fortitude, prowess ____________

(d) potency, zeal, vitality ____________

(e) frenzy, frenetic, ardour ____________

(f) tenacious, indefatigable, vehemence ____________

B. CROSSWORD

Across

1. The power of something e.g. a medicine is its ______________ .
2. A person who has a great drive for something is ______________ .
3. If you are hardworking you are ______________ .
4. The courage to bear something is ______________ .
5. Something which happens at a wild pace is ______________ .
6. Somebody who is chirpy, bubbly is ______________ .
7. Vigour and energy is ______________ .

Down

1. Cutting and sharp e.g. wit is ______________ .
2. Passion for something is ______________ .
3. Someone who has manly strength is ______________ .
4. Mad excitement at a party is ______________ .
5. Endurance for something is ______________ .
6. Skill and expertise is ______________ .

1. T
1. P
2. A
2. Z
3.
3. V
4. F
5. F
5. T
6. P
6. V
7. V

Ch: 7 DIFFICULT OR TOUGH, SECRETIVE OR HIDDEN —Can't quite figure it out!

ABSTRUSE hard to understand (adj)

How it is used: She had thought her thesis would turn out to be profound and scholarly but it turned out to be so **abstruse** that it defied explanation.

My link:

I was told by the teacher to not write my project report in my characteristic **abstruse** manner.

ADAMANT inflexible, not ready to change mind (adj)

How it is used: Young Philip was **adamant** about visiting his biological parents, not trying to understand the complexity of the situation.

My link:

When I got some money, I was **adamant** about buying a pair of expensive shoes, not caring if my parents approved of it or not.

ARCANE understood by few, mysterious (adj)

How it is used: Many old societies and civilizations had certain rituals and religious practices which now look **arcane** and obscure.

My link:

ARDUOUS — difficult and tiring (adj)

How it is used: Going up and down the mountains daily can be quite an **arduous** task even for the hill-people.

My link:

CAMOUFLAGE — hide or disguise (v)

How it is used: Nature has given several tactics and mechanisms of **camouflaging** to creatures in order to escape their enemies.

My link:

CLANDESTINE — secretive, surreptitious (adj)

How it is used: Her **clandestine** affairs with many young men earned her quite an infamous reputation in the small town.

My link:

CONCEALMENT — hiding or prevention (n)

How it is used: **Concealment** of important facts or details can lead to impeachment of court.

My link:

CONUNDRUM a confusing or difficult problem (n)

How it is used: Furthering the developments of science in the field of genetics and maintaining the balance of ethics and morality is turning out to be quite a **conundrum.**

My link:

CONVOLUTED complex (as in a story or argument) (adj)

How it is used: With many plots and subplots, the story became so **convoluted** that by the time the little readers reached half-way, they got completely confused.

My link:

CRUX a particular point of difficulty (n)

How it is used: When the system crashed, the whole team got down to get to the **crux** of the problem.

My link:

CRYPTIC mysterious, obscure (adj)

How it is used: During wartime it is common to send **cryptic** messages to prevent sensitive information from falling in enemy's hands.

My link:

DEADLOCK a situation where no progress can be made (n)

How it is used: Right at the moment when the deal was to be finalised, the negotiations broke down and ended in a **deadlock**.

My link:

DRACONIAN harsh or severe (mainly laws) (adj)

How it is used: In order to curb the rising student unrest, the authorities took some **draconian** steps instead of talking to the students.

My link:

ENCUMBRANCE burden, impediment (n)

How it is used: If only Anne had realised that those two huge suitcases she was carrying would prove to be such an **encumbrance**, she would have travelled light.

My link:

ENIGMATIC obscure, ambiguous, mysterious (adj)

How it is used: Studying human mind, how the brain is structured, and how it works, can be very **enigmatic.**

My link:

ENSCONCE establish in a comfortable, secret place (v)

How it is used: As soon as the newly elected President was properly **ensconced** in the position, she decided to take on her critics and detractors.

My link:

ESOTERIC difficult to understand, meant for people with specialised knowledge or interest (adj)

How it is used: Making weird designs in the fashion fraternity gives one the label of an **esoteric** designer, of someone who has arrived.

My link:

FASTIDIOUS difficult to please, very particular about details, accuracy, cleanliness etc. (adj)

How it is used: Their son was so **fastidious** that he wanted his clothes ironed in a particular way, his food served in a special way.

My link:

FORMIDABLE impressive, powerful (adj)

How it is used: Though little Tim was really small, his courage and wisdom were much more **formidable** for his age.

My link:

IMBROGLIO — a confused or complicated situation (n)

How it is used: What had started as a harmless practical joke, initiated by Calvin on his friend John, soon engulfed everyone in the group, and became quite an **imbroglio**.

My link:

IMPALPABLE — not easily understood or felt (adj)

How it is used: Her pulse was increasingly turning **impalpable** and lips were becoming blue.

My link:

IMPASSÈ — a deadlock, situation of no hope (n)

How it is used: Though the talks had gone on for long between the warring sides, the **impassè** could not be broken.

My link:

IMPEDE — to make progress difficult, to create hurdle (v)

How it is used: To not provide facilities and support material is equal to **impeding** someone's progress.

My link:

IMPERVIOUS

not letting anything pass (e.g. a fluid) impenetrable, tough (adj)

How it is used:

In the world of fashion, modelling and acting, one can survive if one becomes **impervious** to peeping eyes, criticism & bad publicity.

My link:

IMPLACABLE

relentless, unable to be pleased (adj.)

How it is used:

The child had already cried a lot and was still implacable, even by the parents.

My link:

INSCRUTABLE

impossible to understand (adj)

How it is used:

Inspite of knowing the Mayor well, lot of people found him **inscrutable**, as they could never figure out what was behind that stone face.

My link:

INTRANSIGENT

unwilling to agree or change one's views, stubborn (adj)

How it is used:

The situation was becoming more difficult as the kidnappers were totally **intransigent** about their demands and not ready to negotiate at all.

My link:

LABYRYNTHINE complicated, twisted (adj)

How it is used: The children were excitedly lost in the **labyrynthine** passages and alleys of the many famous castles on their tour of Scotland.

My link:

LATENT hidden, existing but not developed (adj)

How it is used: It was amazing how much talent the boy had for playing chess, something which was **latent** and no one had discovered yet.

My link:

MASQUERADE a false show, to be disguised (n)

How it is used: The whole fashion show was based on the theme of a **masquerade** ball of the Elizabethan times.

My link:

NONPLUSSED unperturbed (v)

How it is used: The veteran actor seemed to be **nonplussed** at the heaps of criticism that came his way after the release of his new movie.

My link:

OBDURATE stubborn, hard (adj)

How it is used: The Principal was **obdurate** in his decision of suspending the agitating students at the university.

My link:

OBFUSCATE to make unclear or unintelligible (v)

How it is used: The last resort of the police force, when they can't solve a case, is to **obfuscate** it, so as to confound the public.

My link:

OBLIVION forgetfulness, unawareness (n)

How it is used: What were once the pride of every country, the native languages are slowly falling into **oblivion**.

My link:

OBSCURE difficult and hidden (v)

How it is used: A lot of literature students find "The Wasteland" by T.S. Eliot, an **obscure** piece of poetry.

My link:

OBTRUDE to impose, to intrude (v)

How it is used: So as not to **obtrude** in their young children's privacy, parents find it difficult to keep communication going and yet maintain a distance.

My link:

OBVIATE remove (a need or difficulty), avoid (v)

How it is used: Once a problem has been identified and the need to tackle it has been established, it is not difficult to **obviate** it.

My link:

ONEROUS burdensome and difficult (adj)

How it is used: Shifting houses every now and then proved too **onerous** a task for her.

My link:

ONUS burden, duty (n)

How it is used: In a democracy the **onus** of selecting capable leaders lies on the people.

My link:

PREDICAMENT a difficult situation (n)

How it is used: Having given her word to the boss about the completion of the project on time, she was in a terrible **predicament** of finishing her work, or attending the wedding in the family.

My link:

QUANDARY to be uncertain, undecided, not knowing what to do in a difficult situation (n)

How it is used: Isabelle was in a **quandary** to continue her job in New York or accompany her husband to Chicago.

My link:

RECLUSE leading a solitary life (n)

How it is used: Everyone knew that the retired diplomat led the life of a **recluse** after his wife's death, so no one in the neighbourhood came to know that he had been shot by an armed robber, the night before.

My link:

RECONDITE obscure (adj)

How it is used: Milton's Paradise Lost is a **recondite** piece of poetry, involving several facets of morality, mythology and theology.

My link:

STALEMATE a deadlock (n)

How it is used: Inspite of making all efforts to break the **stalemate**, the two countries could not be brought to sign a treaty over the border dispute.

My link:

UNCANNY strange, mysterious (adj)

How it is used: She had never set foot outside her country, yet she could speak several languages without any formal training, and she was the talk of the town for this **uncanny** ability.

My link:

PRACTICE EXERCISE

Fill in the grid with the correct options in the blank spaces.

WORDS	SYNONYMS	ANTONYMS
1. uncanny	mysterious	____________
2. stalemate	____________	a solvable situation
3. recondite	difficult to understand	____________
4. recluse	____________	social, extrovert
5. quandary	____________	easy situation
6. predicament	difficult situation	____________
7. onus	responsibility	____________
8. onerous	burdensome	____________
9. obviate	____________	create need of
10. obtrude	impose	____________
11. obscure	hidden	____________
12. oblivion	forgetfulness	____________
13. obfuscate	confuse	____________
14. obdurate	stubborn	____________
15. nonplussed	unmoved	____________
16. masquerade	____________	true character
17. latent	____________	obvious
18. labyrynthine	____________	simple, straight
19. intransigent	stubborn	____________
20. inscrutable	difficult to solve	____________
21. implacable	difficult to please	____________
22. impervious	____________	penetrable
23. impede	obstruct	____________
24. impassè	____________	hope of being solved
25. impalpable	____________	clearly understood

WORDS	SYNONYMS	ANTONYMS
26. imbroglio	________	disentanglement
27. formidable	________	unimpressive
28. fastidious	squeamish	
29. esoteric	________	common place
30. ensconce	________	expose
31. enigmatic	mysterious	________
32. encumbrance	________	hassle free
33. draconian	________	lenient
34. deadlock	________	solvable
35. cryptic	________	easy, simple
36. crux	________	not so important
37. convoluted	complicated	________
38. conundrum	confusing and difficult	________
39. concealment	hiding away	________
40. clandestine	________	open
41. camouflage	________	expose
42. arduous	________	not-exerting
43. arcane	________	obvious
44. adamant	________	flexible
45. abstruse	profound	________

REVIEW EXERCISE–1

Choose the word which fits in best in the given blank in each sentence.

reclusive, formidable, crux, cryptic, imbroglio, impediment, impervious, unobtrusive, obfuscated, ensconced, arcane, esoteric, onerous, predicament, obviate, obdurate, concealed, inscrutable, latent, clandestine, adamant, uncanny, impalpable, draconian, fastidious

1. He replied to my questions in such a __________ manner that I could hardly understand anything.
2. If only he could realise that it was his own negative thinking that was the biggest __________ in his progress.
3. The __________ of the entire environmental crisis is people's inability to change their lifestyle.
4. She had become so __________ to anybody's advice that no one's pleadings moved her.
5. Winning over her parent's approval for a biking tour around the world was quite a ______ task.
6. They thought they were safely __________ in the underground bunkers till the bombings started ripping the neighbourhood apart.
7. The __________ hermit hardly made any appearance except for an occasional demand for food and water.
8. It was quite obvious that the issue had been deliberately __________ so that nobody could reach to the core of the problem.
9. The bilateral dialogues between the two countries delegations turned into an __________ with both sides accusing each other of cross-border terrorism.
10. In one scene the prompting done by the actors on stage was handled in such an __________ manner that it looked like a part of the original script.
11. The popularity of computers has __________ the need of many traditional tools like a typewriter, office files, mounds of paper etc.
12. Shifting houses or getting them painted can be an __________ task, particularly for working couples.
13. The __________ stand of the company's CEO on the merger, cost the company dearly.
14. John had a tough __________, he could neither leave his job, nor did he want to move to the other city, where the company was relocating.

15. In childhood his fascination for strange drawings and phenomena drew him towards the __________ as he grew, and made him famous as an abstract painter.

16. Lot of stuff which was earlier considered __________ and inexplicable has now been defined by science.

17. Children born in poverty have many __________ abilities which are never nurtured because of lack of opportunities.

18. The two of them had never met before, were not related and yet were so similar that it was __________.

19. Debbie was __________ about marrying John, even though she knew what a big liar he was.

20. Sebi was increasingly becoming more irritable and depressive though the problem seemed __________ to everyone around her.

21. Nancy's mother was so __________ about keeping the house clean and in order that she even stopped the children from playing outside, lest they made the house dirty with their muddy footprints.

22. As societies advanced, a lot of __________laws of the past had to be revoked or modified to give way to a more liberal order.

23. The __________ deal of the merger was exposed to the press by a disgruntled employee.

24. The opening to the cave was so well __________ that it reminded the explorers of the Ali Baba and Forty Thieves legend.

25. Several problems in the Mathematics exam were found to be __________ even by the brilliant students.

REVIEW EXERCISE–2

Given in front of each word is an option which could either be a synonym or an antonym or none. Choose the right option and put S or A or N for each of the above given choices. First one has been done for you.

1. quandary	confusion, uncertainty	S
2. concealment	be exposed	
3. obscurity	oblivion	
4. encumbrance	hinderance	
5. arduous	easy, simple	
6. obdurate	negative	
7. camouflage	disappear	
8. convoluted	complicated	
9. stalemate	deadlock	
10. impediment	hurdle-free	
11. recondite	easy to understand	
12. conundrum	confusion	
13. clandestine	openly	
14. labyrinth	spherical	
15. enigma	mystery	
16. latent	obvious	
17. draconian	severe	
18. impalpable	clear	
19. fastidious	easy going	
20. arcane	old fashioned	

Ch: 8 ENVIRONMENT —Saving it is now or never

ARID dry, uninteresting (adj)

How it is used: Thanks to indiscriminate cutting of trees, more and more land is turning **arid**.

My link:

When it did not rain in our area for several years, we had great difficulty in learning to survive in those **arid** conditions.

BUCOLIC pastoral, of rural life (adj)

How it is used: Very soon **bucolic** life will become a rarity, as the whole world will be living in cities.

My link:

When I visited my grand aunt at her quaint village, I was charmed by the **bucolic** sights of green meadows and farms.

CARRION decaying flesh of dead animals (n)

How it is used: Vultures are now being considered to be vital to ecological balance because they are nature's way of removing **carrion** by eating it.

My link:

EPHEMERAL lasting or living for a short time (adj)

How it is used: The spring this time seemed to be very **ephemeral**, quickly turning into a hot summer very soon.

My link:

FORAGE search widely for food (v)

How it is used: **Foraging** for food was primitive man's main occupation.

My link:

HALCYON happy and peaceful times of past (adj)

How it is used: Who doesn't miss the **halcyon** days of their youth, when life seemed to be so carefree and idyllic.

My link:

MEANDER follow a winding course (of a river or road) (v)

How it is used: If you are lost in a tropical jungle, follow the **meandering** river to get out.

My link:

MENAGERIE collection of wild animals (n)

How it is used: As the students trooped back into the classes after the vacations, the whole campus buzzed like a **menagerie**.

My link:

METEORIC very rapid (change or development) (adj)

How it is used: Given his charm and wit, no one was surprised at his **meteoric** rise in the film industry.

My link:

MIASMA unpleasant atmosphere (n)

How it is used: When the sun shone after continuous rain, the city streets were still flooded and the whole place seemed to be a **miasma** of stench and decay.

My link:

MIRAGE optical illusion caused by atmospheric conditions (n)

How it is used: Many a thirsty traveller has lost his life in the desert due to the appearance of water, which turns out to be only a **mirage**.

My link:

NADIR lowest point, most unsuccessful point (n)

How it is used: When he got heavily into drugs, it was the **nadir** of the actor's career.

My link:

NEBULOUS cloudy or hazy (adj)

How it is used: Because of the occurrence of a near total solar eclipse, the atmosphere looked **nebulous**, when it should have been a bright sunshiny afternoon otherwise.

My link:

NOCTURNAL done or active at night (adj)

How it is used: Mrs. Wilson became used to Mr. Wilson's **nocturnal** visits to the fridge for midnight snacks.

My link:

OBSIDIAN hard, dark volcanic rock (n)

How it is used: The whole landscape was full of interesting formations of **obsidian**, shining like glass in the sunlight.

My link:

PACHYDERM large mammals with thick skin. e.g. rhinos, elephants, hippos etc. (n)

How it is used: If enough forests do not remain on earth, the dwindling **pachyderm** population might just disappear.

My link:

PANORAMIC large expansive view (adj)

How it is used: She captured the **panoramic** view of the entire valley, very beautifully in her camera.

My link:

PERENNIAL lasting through the year, enduring (adj)

How it is used: Due to indiscriminate use of their waters, many **perennial** rivers are now drying up in summers.

My link:

PIEBALD mottled, of different colours (adj)

How it is used: Whether it was a nature's gift or a freak case, their pet dog had an interesting **piebald** appearance.

My link:

PLUMAGE — bird's feathers collectively (n)

How it is used: Several kinds of tropical cockatoos have been identified mainly by their distinctive **plumage**.

My link:

PRECIPITOUS — dangerously high or steep, sudden or dramatic (as in change) (adj)

How it is used: Everybody was amazed at the **precipitous** rise of his company's share values.

My link:

PROLIFERATE — reproduce/increase rapidly (v)

How it is used: If slums are allowed to **proliferate** indiscriminately, they become a drain on cities' resources.

My link:

PUTRID — unpleasant, rotting smell (adj)

How it is used: The **putrid** stench coming from the house indicated that the dead body had been lying there for weeks.

My link:

QUAGMIRE soft boggy area of land/complex situation (n)

How it is used: Steeped in debt, Mr. Grunge did not know how to get out of the **quagmire** that he himself had created.

My link:

RAMIFICATION branches, consequence of an action or event (n)

How it is used: The **ramifications** of increasing radicalisation of societies and countries are many.

My link:

REDOLENT strongly smelling of/strongly reminiscent of (adj)

How it is used: It is a pleasure to walk through the parks in springtime, because the air is **redolent** with sweet fragrance of flowers.

My link:

SALVAGE rescue (a ship or its cargo), retrieve from loss (v)

How it is used: Various efforts made to **salvage** the deepening political crisis before World War II had failed.

My link:

SCAVENGE search for and collect (anything usable) from garbage, discarded things (v)

How it is used: Lot of people have a hobby of **scavenging** for antique furnitures and collectibles in flea markets.

My link:

SEISMIC relating to earthquakes (adj)

How it is used: Birds and animals are very quick to perceive even the slightest indication of any **seismic** disturbances.

My link:

SIMIAN relating to apes or monkeys (adj)

How it is used: Many animals of the **simian** category are gradually becoming extinct.

My link:

SINEWY tough, muscular (adj)

How it is used: The cheetah in the zoo charmed everyone with its lithe and **sinewy** body.

My link:

STRATUM — layer of earth's surface, layer of society (n)

How it is used: It is unfortunate that the benefit of various social welfare schemes never reach the **stratum** for which they are meant.

My link:

TEMPESTUOUS — stormy, turbulent emotion (adj)

How it is used: Her **tempestuous** nature turned her children into cowering fearful creatures.

The **tempestuous** sea tossed and turned the ship like a toy.

My link:

TERRESTRIAL — relating to earth or land (adj)

How it is used: **Terrestrial** occurrences are easy to study and document as compared to extra-terrestrial happenings.

My link:

TETHERED — tied by rope or chain (an animal) (v)

How it is used: The camels were tired after the long journey through the desert, and so were **tethered** to the tents for the night.

My link:

TORRID hot and dry (intense emotions arising out of passion) (adj)

How it is used:

- The **torrid** weather extended far longer than normal and caused many forest fires.
- The **torrid** affairs of Madam Bovary are famous in English literature.

My link:

TURBID Cloudy, opaque, confused (adj)

How it is used: The otherwise clear waters of the lake looked **turbid** after the storm and heavy rain.

My link:

TURGID swollen, pompous (adj)

How it is used: Three days of continuous rain turned the river into a **turgid** menace.

My link:

UNDULATING wavy form of surface (adj)

How it is used: Scotland is full of **undulating** meadows and grassy hills.

My link:

VERDURE green lush vegetation (n)

How it is used: The **verdure** of the meadows in the countryside was really soothing.

My link:

VERNAL spring season (adj)

How it is used: Earlier **vernal** temperatures used to be low but now its turning hotter and hotter even as early as February and March.

My link:

ZENITH highest point in the sky, most successful stage (n)

How it is used: Many people can't handle fame and fortune, and destroy their success at its **zenith**.

My link:

ZEPHYR soft gentle breeze (n)

How it is used: The blue of the Mediterranean sea and the pleasant **zephyr** made sailing in the yatch a unique experience.

My link:

PRACTICE EXERCISE

Fill in the grid with the correct options in the blank spaces.

WORDS	SYNONYMS	ANTONYMS
1. zephyr	gentle breeze	___________
2. zenith	___________	nadir
3. vernal	___________	autumnal
4. undulating	___________	flat
5. turgid	___________	abated
6. turbid	___________	transparent
7. torrid	passionate	___________
8. tethered	tied	___________
9. terrestrial	___________	aerial
10. tempestuous	stormy	___________
11. sinewy	tough	___________
12. scavenge	search	___________
13. salvage	rescue	___________
14. redolent	___________	without smell
15. ramification	___________	cause
16. quagmire	complex	___________
17. putrid	___________	sweet smelling
18. proliferate	multiply	___________
19. precipitous	___________	sloping
20. pie-bald	___________	plain, monochromatic
21. perennial	___________	seasonal

WORDS	SYNONYMS	ANTONYMS
22. panoramic	______________	small, limited
23. nocturnal	______________	diurnal
24. nadir	lowest point	______________
25. mirage	illusion	______________
26. miasma	unpleasant	______________
27. meteoric	______________	slow
28. meandering	______________	straight
29. maelstrom	______________	clear, precise
30. forage	______________	N/A
31. arid	______________	arable

N/A: Not applicable

REVIEW EXERCISE–1

Given along with each sentence are three words. Choose the option which fits in best in the given blanks in the sentence.

1. The mountain's peak was not only treacherously ____________ but also inhospitable and rugged. (undulating, precipitous, pristine)
2. Many a poets have written indulgently about the charms of ____________ season. (vernal, putrid, verdure)
3. Unless all ____________ of society benefit from the boom in economy the reforms are only half-successful. (strata, panorama, zenith)
4. Elephants are the most intelligent of all ____________. (simian, plumage, pachyderms)
5. As soon as the news of fire broke out in the cinema theatre, there was a complete ____________ with people running here and there in panic. (verdure, maelstrom, quagmire)
6. Her cottage had bay windows which when opened gave a ____________ view of the sea. (panoramic, perennial, putrid)
7. The pollution in the river was so extreme that even the air around it smelt ____________. (turgid, turbid, putrid)
8. As long as they were together they had a ____________ affair, but soon both tired of each other and moved their own ways. (tempestuous, verdure, redolent)
9. The park was ____________ with the memories of her children who were now grown up and gone. (redolent, proliferate, mirage)
10. Their cow Daisy had a very interesting ____________ appearance. (vernal, pie-bald, tethered)
11. Several top quality horses were ____________ to their posts in the stables of Mr. Grisham at his stud farm. (foraged, tethered, scavenged)
12. The ____________ arms of Mr. Scot indicated how hard he had worked on the farms all his life. (pristine sinewy, nocturnal)
13. ____________ activities below the water in oceans and seas cause greater damage than earthquakes on land. (carrion, terrestrial, seismic)
14. Imagine a situation where earth is hit by a nuclear disaster and mankind is destroyed and few who have survived are left to ____________ for food and water. (forage, scavenge salvage)
15. It is alarming that more and more area, of what was once fertile land, is now turning into ____________ useless soil. (redolent, arid, quagmire)

16. Having been lost in the wilderness for the past five days, the lone traveller did not know if the sight of human habitation was a __________ or real. (ramification, nebula, mirage)
17. Inter-tribal rivalry, vested interest of developed countries and political turmoil have turned several African countries into a __________ of corruption and violence. (miasma, nadir, zenith)
18. Forests are never quiet, even at night the __________ creatures are up and about. (nocturnal, perennial, panoramic)
19. Everyone knew he had brains, but his rise would be so __________ surprised many. (meandering, meteoric, mirage)
20. The rainbow was so __________ that by the time the children gathered it was gone. (mirage, nebulous, ephemeral)

REVIEW EXERCISE–2

Given below are some definitions in column A. In column B some words are given in jumbled order. Match the words with the given definitions which best describe the word.

Column A	Column B
1. Expansive, comprehensive view	(a) nebulous
2. Optical illusion	(b) zephyr
3. Complicated situation	(c) undulating
4. Fragrant	(d) nadir
5. Consequences of an action	(e) sinewy
6. Wavy or uneven	(f) turgid
7. Search for something	(g) ramification
8. Relating to earth	(h) panoramic
9. Relating to monkeys	(i) ephemeral
10. Stormy	(j) simian
11. Soft gentle breeze	(k) obsidion
12. Swollen	(l) quagmire
13. Highest point in the sky	(m) scavenge
14. Lowest point in the sky	(n) terrestrial
15. Tough muscular	(o) tempestuous
16. Cloudy	(p) mirage
17. Volcanic rock	(q) redolent
18. short-lasting	(r) zenith

Ch: 9

EVIL
—Get out of harm's way

AVARICE extreme greed for wealth/material gains (n)

How it is used: Sometimes it appears true that man is plundering the earth for his **avarice**.

My link:

My mother told me very early in childhood that I should not be **avaricious** towards others' toys because I couldn't buy everything.

CALLOUS insensitive and cruel (adj)

How it is used: The **callous** attitude of the government towards the student leaders' demands turned them into a rampaging mob.

My link:

I will be truthful and admit that sometimes I was callous towards my baby-brother and would let him cry.

CALUMNY false defamatory statements about someone (n)

How it is used: By the time Roger was charged with **calumny** against the art dealer, the dealer himself died.

My link:

CASTIGATE scold severely/punish (v)

How it is used: Several eminent people have been **castigated** in their lifetime for their unconventional thoughts and then honoured after their death.

My link:

DEMONIC devilish (adj)

How it is used: Modern warfare is coming with more **demonic** ways of fighting and torture.

My link:

DEVIANT diverging from accepted behaviour or standard (adj)

How it is used: Initially the parents ignored their son's **deviant** behaviour but soon realised that it was getting out of hand.

My link:

DIABOLIC associated with the devil/unpleasant (adj)

How it is used: Soon enough her **diabolic** attempts at breaking her best friend's marriage, lay exposed.

My link:

FIEND — evil spirit/extremely cruel/demon like (n)

How it is used: When drunk, he left all his decency behind and turned into a **fiend**.

My link:

HEDONIST — pursuit of pleasure/sensual self-indulgence (n)

How it is used: In his lifetime he had been a complete **hedonist** disregarding his family's needs or desires.

My link:

HEINOUS — absolutely hateful, wicked (adj)

How it is used: History is witness to several **heinous** crimes committed by kings and warriors, leaders and nobility.

My link:

INSIDIOUS — proceeding in a gradual harmful way (adj)

How it is used: Her **insidious** efforts at extricating valuable information from the company for a rival organisation, cost her job.

My link:

INSTIGATE incite someone to do something (bad) (v)

How it is used: There is always a likelihood of somebody else having **instigated** riots between two groups or communities.

My link:

MACHIAVELEAN cunning, scheming (in politics or business) (adj)

How it is used: It is true that people who have a **machiavelean** temperament are extremely successful as politicians.

My link:

MALEFIC causing harm/having evil influence (adj)

How it is used: In medieval times, several women were tortured because they were considered to be witches who had **malefic** influence on people.

My link:

MALEVOLENT wishing evil to others (adj)

How it is used: **Malevolent** streaks in a person's nature, wreak havoc in his own life, sooner or later.

My link:

MANIACAL — showing wild/violent behaviour (adj)

How it is used: It was widely believed in the area that the old mansion was haunted by the spirit of a woman and people had even heard her **maniacal** laughter.

My link:

MISANTHROPE — a person who dislikes humankind (n)

How it is used: Is it alright to call terrorists, **misanthropes** because they are misguided about their mission and purpose.

My link:

MISCREANT — one who behaves badly or unlawfully, villain (n)

How it is used: It was difficult to say if the damage done to the shop was the handiwork of some local **miscreants** or was a planned attack.

My link:

NEFARIOUS — wicked or criminal (adj)

How it is used: It was unbelievable how the very gentle next-door Bob had turned into a **nefarious** criminal.

My link:

PERNICIOUS destructive, harmful in a slow manner (adj)

How it is used: Scientists are now realising that the danger to the environment may be more **pernicious** than thought earlier and also irreversible in certain ways.

My link:

PIQUE feel irritated or resentful (n or v)

How it is used: She showed her **pique** at the grandeur of the party because she knew she could not compete with it.

My link:

QUISLING traitor (n)

How it is used: Many a kingdom has fallen not so much at the hands of enemies as at the hands of **quislings**.

My link:

RENEGADE someone who betrays an organisation, country, religion etc. (n)

How it is used: In the eyes of the government he was a **renegade**, but in the eyes of the local people, he was a hero, who upheld their cause and their rights.

My link:

SADIST someone who derives pleasure from inflicting pain on others (n)

How it is used: It was revealed much later that the military general was a **sadist** and derived pleasure from the death of his own soldiers in mock gun battles.

My link:

TIRADE long speech of criticism (n)

How it is used: When scolding children, one should not go into lengthy **tirades**, but focus only on the wrongful act or problem at hand.

My link:

TRUCULENT aggressively defiant (adj)

How it is used: Her **truculent** nature not only destroyed her marriage, but also her mental equilibrium.

My link:

TURPITUDE depravity, wickedness (n)

How it is used: Moral **turpitude** is slowly becoming the order of the day.

My link:

UNSCRUPULOUS — without moral principles (adj)

How it is used: The mutiliated body showed that the murder had been done in a completely **unscrupulous** manner.

My link:

VINDICTIVE — extremely revengeful (adj)

How it is used: Being **vindictive** is the easiest, it is forgiving and moving on, that is most difficult.

My link:

VIRULENT — extremely severe or harmful in effect, hostile (adj)

How it is used: Seeing the divorce case not going in her favour, the estranged wife became extremely **virulent**.

My link:

VITIATE — destroy, impair, spoil the effect of (v)

How it is used: It was with great difficulty that the two warring sides had agreed to a ceasefire, but as soon the news of two deaths were reported, the atmosphere again got **vitiated**.

My link:

PRACTICE EXERCISE

Now let us see if you are able to recognise the words you have learnt in this chapter. A brief definition and the first letter have been given for your help. First one has been done for you.

1. A word associated with hateful crime — Heinous ______________
2. To deliberately harm someone is being — I ______________
3. Someone who's a traitor is a — Q ______________
4. Behaving madly is being — M ______________
5. Being revengeful is being — V ______________
6. Something associated with devil is — D ______________
7. Extremely cruel and devilish is — F ______________
8. Someone ready to fight or defy is — T ______________
9. When you incite someone to do wrong you — I ______________
10. Excessive greed for wealth is — A ______________
11. Having no scruples, or principles is — U ______________
12. When you feel resentful you are — P ______________
13. Someone indulging in sensual pleasure is a — H ______________
14. Moral depravity is — T ______________
15. When you scold or punish severely you — C ______________
16. A person who hates mankind is a — M ______________
17. A person who creates trouble is a — M ______________
18. To spoil or destroy something is to — V ______________
19. A dangerous harmful situation is what becomes — V ______________
20. A criminal indulges in these activities — N ______________

REVIEW EXERCISE–1

Some words are given below which mean the opposite to the following definitions given. Choose the right word and write in the corresponding blank.

misanthrope, castigate, avarice, calumny, truculent, malefic, pernicious, unscrupulous, hedonist, instigate, insidious, malevolent, callous, pique, tirade

1. Having a good influence M ____________
2. To spread goodwill for someone C ____________
3. Benevolent M ____________
4. Harmless and beneficial P ____________
5. Quieten and improve the situation I ____________
6. Obedient, friendly and quiet T ____________
7. Having strong morals U ____________
8. A saint who gives up pleasure H ____________
9. Appreciate and reward C ____________
10. No desire for material possessions A ____________
11. Kind and sensitive C ____________
12. To please someone P ____________
13. helpful and supportive I ____________
14. Long speech of praise T ____________
15. Philanthropic and kind M ____________

REVIEW EXERCISE–2

Below are given some sentences with blanks. Choose the correct word from the list of words given and fill in the blanks appropriately.

callously, fiend, vindictive, malefic, malevolence, calumny, sadist, pernicious, machiavelean, virulent, hedonistic, insidious, avarice, piqued, nefarious, turpitude, unscrupulous, instigated, maniacally, castigated, diabolic, heinous, quisling, truculent, renegade.

1. The small townspeople had a narrow mentality and felt that the new vicar was having a ____________ influence because his preachings had scientific and modern logic which they could not understand.
2. One needs to have ____________ tendencies to make money out of situations of human disaster, and cheat poor victims also.
3. Serena's ____________ was evident when she actually tried to set fire to the clothes of her ex-boyfriend's fiance.
4. The young lawyer was alleged to be indulging in ____________ against the millionaire by accusing him of bribery and forgery.
5. The boy had been brought up by wolves in the jungle since he was a baby and behaved ____________ and wildly just like them.
6. The after-effects of the atom-bomb explosion turned out to more ____________ than they were initially thought to be.
7. Martin had left the army to join the revolutionaries, who called him their leader, while army top brass wanted to gun him down as he was a ____________ .
8. As modern medicines tend to be more potent, even disease viruses are becoming ____________ and drug resistant.
9. Everyone knew that Jacob lost all his fortune because of the ____________ nature of his ex-wife.
10. The local don was feared by one and all for his ____________ deeds.
11. What happens if a saviour himself turns into a ____________ and starts abusing the very people he is supposed to protect?
12. The baby cried seeing his drunk father behave like a ____________ .
13. Instead of sending relief to the drought stricken people the ministry ____________ indulged in political mud-slinging.
14. The castle which was thought to be invincible fell to the enemies because of one ____________.
15. He was stricken with a most horrific disease, and people said he was paying the price for his ____________ lifestyle in his youth.

16. The parishioner gave sermon on the topic of moral ____________ when incidents of robberies increased in the once-quiet village.

17. Calista was ____________ by her family because she had denounced the family tradition of being a nurse and rather joined the world of glamour as an actress.

18. Terrorist attacks are becoming more and more ____________ as they have now begun to target places where there is maximum human concentration.

19. Several ____________ crimes have been committed in the name of religion.

20. What she said was even more ____________ than what she did.

21. When tempers cooled down, it became apparent that the fight had been ____________ by outsiders who had been hired to create trouble.

22. Can all violence and plundering be attributed to one human vice—____________?

23. The secessionists were known for their ____________ speeches which always lead people to blindly believe in the cause of their motherland.

24. Robina's arrest made her feel ____________ because she had laid a well-thought out plan to murder her husband and become an heiress to his millions.

25. Lady Macbeth is considered to be an ____________ lady who brought about so much of destruction.

Ch: 10

FOOD —Hungry for more

AMBROSIA — food for Gods, very pleasing to taste or smell (n)

How it is used: For the lost and weary travellers, the smell of food being cooked, coming from a hut in the forest was like **ambrosia**.

My link:

When I come home from college, food made by my mother tastes like **ambrosia**.

BLANCH — make or become white or pale (v)

How it is used: Though people suspected the young widow of having an affair, she looked **blanched** out of grief for her husband's death.

My link:

At the cooking class I was asked to **blanch** the almonds and slice them into thin slivers before putting them into the pudding.

CONDIMENTS — flavourings such as salt, pepper, spices etc. (n)

How it is used: The **condiments** that went into her dishes to make them so delicious, were her trade secrets.

My link:

CUISINE a style or method of cooking (n)

How it is used: In India, it is said, that language and **cuisine** change every 500 kms.

My link:

DELECTABLE delicious, delightful (adj)

How it is used: The spread at the country feast organised by our hosts consisted of several **delectable** meat and vegetable dishes.

My link:

EPICUREAN a person who enjoys fine food and drink (n)

How it is used: These days it is trendy to have fine-dining restaurants for the **epicureans** and the elite.

My link:

GARNISH decorate or embellish especially food (v)

How it is used: Great chefs believe in **garnishing** the food as painstakingly as preparing it.

My link:

GLUTTONY habitual greed or excess in eating (n)

How it is used: Howsoever he was teased for **gluttony**, it did not reduce his appetite or change his habit.

My link:

GOURMAND a person who enjoys eating (n)

How it is used: Only a **gourmand** can become a successful food critic, as he/she will never tire of his/her work.

My link:

GOURMET conoisseur of good food (n)

How it is used: The **gourmet** restaurant did a thriving business in the upmarket area.

My link:

LEAVEN to transform for better, cause to ferment and rise by adding yeast (v)

How it is used: The trick to producing perfect bread is to **leaven** it properly.

My link:

MANNA food from heaven, an unexpected benefit (n)

How it is used: For flood-victims the food packets being dropped by the helicopters, were actually like **manna**.

My link:

MASTICATE chew nicely (v)

How it is used: **Masticating** food well, the way the cattle do, is the key to good digestion.

My link:

PIQUANT pleasantly sharp tasting, or stimulating (adj)

How it is used:

- Europeans for centuries have valued Indian spices for their **piquant** taste and flavour.
- The group discussion with the intellectuals lent a **piquant** flavour to the entire congregation.

My link:

POTABLE fit for drinking (adj)

How it is used: The whole world is going to face acute shortage of **potable** water, because very soon all sources of fresh water would have either dried up or been polluted.

My link:

PUNGENT strong taste or smell (adj)

How it is used: Sometimes too much of garlic in food can make it too **pungent** to be relished.

My link:

RAVENOUS extremely hungry (adj)

How it is used: After the long uphill trek, the climbers were exhausted and **ravenous**.

My link:

SATIATE fully satisfy (v)

How it is used: Its difficult to **satiate** one's thirst on a hot summer afternoon of a tropical country.

My link:

SCRUMPTIOUS extremely appetizing or delicious (adj)

How it is used: The people at the party wondered that if the appetizers were so **scrumptious**, what would the main course be like.

My link:

TEPID — lukewarm, unenthusiastic (adj)

How it is used: The water was just **tepid** enough to bathe the baby.

Contrary to his expectations, the welcome he received was quite **tepid** and laboured.

My link:

VIANDS — an item of food (n)

How it is used: The famine forced the poor people to beg for some **viands** in the rich peoples' streets.

My link:

VICTUALS — foods or provisions (n)

How it is used: The least humans can do is to provide **victuals** to the poor, hungry and needy.

My link:

VORACIOUS — eagerly consuming something (adj)

How it is used:

- After the wrestling practice he would attack food with a **voracious** appetite.
- He was a **voracious** reader and would read all the titles available.

My link:

PRACTICE EXERCISE

Fill in the grid with the correct options in the blank spaces.

WORDS	SYNONYMS	ANTONYMS
1. voracious	____________	not hungry
2. tepid	____________	excessively hot
3. scrumptious	____________	unappetizing
4. satiate	satisfy	____________
5. ravenous	____________	satiated, full
6. pungent	____________	mild
7. potable	____________	not worth drinking
8. piquant	sharp, stimulating	____________
9. masticate	chew properly	____________
10. leaven	____________	make worse
11. gluttony	greed	____________
12. garnish	decorate	____________
13. delectable	tasty	____________
14. blanch	____________	give colour

REVIEW EXERCISE–1

Choose the word which fits in best in the given blank in each sentence.

cuisine, ambrosia, tepid, ravenous, blanched, mastication, garnishing, delectable, gourmand, victuals, potable, pungent, scrumptious, voraciously, leavened, glutton, piquancy, manna, condiments, epicurean.

1. Some cuisines are known to be having strong and _________ flavours.
2. Under the new king, the condition of the kingdom _________ and things became much better.
3. If it is true that all ailments start from our stomach, then proper _________ of food is necessary to enable proper digestion.
4. Her recipes were generally difficult to follow because they required a long list of _________.
5. Martha was worried because she felt her son was turning into a _________, always demanding food and more food.
6. It was surprising how _________ the hyenas attacked the carcass and finished it completely within minutes.
7. A little bit of _________ with coriander, celery or parsley goes a long way in enhancing taste of the dish and making it look colourful.
8. Emily learned to bake _________ desserts in the cookery class.
9. The croissants in the show window looked extremely inviting and _________ .
10. The _________ of the dish came from the rich plum sauce that had been used as the base.
11. These days almost all _________ restaurants can be found in major cities of the world.
12. She was a true _________ when it came to enjoying exotic dishes.
13. On a hungry stomach, plain food also tastes like _________.
14. A rich man's leftovers can be a poor man's _________.
15. In the poem, An Ancient Mariner, the albatross comes to the sailors for the ____________ that they fed it.
16. Washing wounds in _________ saline water is an effective way of disinfecting them.
17. These days there are portable devices which can make really dirty water _________ through micro filters instantly.
18. The tough mountain-climb coughed up a _________ appetite in the climbers.
19. The convict's face _________ at the sight of the nailing evidence produced by the public prosecutor.
20. The spread at the Michelin starred restaurant in Paris was any ____________ delight.

REVIEW EXERCISE–2

Given in front of each word is an option which could either be a Synonym or an Antonym or None. Choose the right option and put an S or A or N for each of the above given choices. First one has been done for you.

		Answers
1. gourmet	who appreciates good food	S
2. gourmand	who hates eating	
3. manna	food of Gods	
4. ambrosia	food from heaven	
5. tepid	lukewarm	
6. cuisine	bad kind of cooking	
7. ravenous	not hungry	
8. pungent	strong tasting	
9. piquant	stimulating	
10. epicurean	one who dislikes good food	
11. leaven	heighten the taste	
12. masticate	mash nicely	
13. scrumptious	delicious	
14. garnish	embellish	
15. blanch	add colour	
16. delectable	delightful	
17. victuals	pieces	
18. viands	item of food	
19. satiate	dissatisfy	
20. potable	can be easily carried	
21. gluttony	greed (for food)	
22. condiments	compliments	

Ch: 11 GODLY, RELIGIOUS, SPIRITUAL —What's your spiritual quotient?

AGNOSTIC — one who does not believe in the existence of God (n)

How it is used: **Agnostics** take the help of scientists and pragmatists to proclaim that there is no God because there is no evidence to prove that He is.

My link:

One of my uncles is an **agnostic**, and is actually very happy thinking there is no God.

ANOINTING — rubbing with oil as part of a religious ceremony (v)

How it is used: Lot of people came for witnessing the prince's **anointing** ceremony and his accession to the throne.

My link:

I was there for my nephew's **anointing** ceremony.

APOCALYPTIC — prophetic, momentous, catastrophic (adj)

How it is used: Nostrè Damus's **apocalyptic** predictions have stunned the world for their exactness and timing.

My link:

BENEDICTION blessing (n)

How it is used: The local church was packed with the village people who had gathered for the **benediction** ceremony of Laurel, the Mayor's son.

My link:

CANON a general rule or principle, a church decree or law (n)

How it is used: It is difficult to decide if those living by the **canons** of civilized society are right and those abiding by laws of nature are not.

My link:

CATECHISM principles of Christian religion in the form of questions and answers, instruction by question and answers (n)

How it is used: Earlier the method of teaching young children was largely through **catechism**.

My link:

CELESTIAL heavenly (adj)

How it is used: People of certain religions believe in the **celestial** formations and planetary positions which may be responsible for occurrences on earth.

My link:

CONGREGATION a group of people assembled for religious purpose (n)

How it is used: It was horrifying to know that the **congregation** had been attacked by the non-believers to show them down.

My link:

CONSECRATE make or declare sacred (v)

How it is used: Although the new church was built and ready yet the Arch Bishop was not free to come and **consecrate** it.

My link:

CORPOREAL relating to body or material objects (n)

How it is used: In this materialistic and consumerist society the gap between the **corporeal** and the spiritual is becoming increasingly wider.

My link:

HERESY opinion contrary to orthodox religious beliefs (n)

How it is used: In the ancient times whenever some persons tried to speak against the common beliefs they were charged with **heresy** and infamy.

My link:

ICONOCLAST a person who attacks cherished beliefs and institutions (n)

How it is used: Whenever somebody has raised voice against established faiths and creeds, people have called that person as an **iconoclast** and banished such radical views.

My link:

INFIDEL a non-believer (n)

How it is used: For as long as human race has been, there have been instances of torture against **infidels** and people of one faith against other faiths.

My link:

LITANY a kind of petition recited by clergy during prayer, a tedious recital (n)

How it is used: The congregation was moved by the **litany** of the priest for the plight of Tsunami affected people.

My link:

OCCULT supernatural beliefs and practices (n)

How it is used: Lots of tribal faiths are based on **occult** and Nature worship.

My link:

OMNISCIENT knowing everything (n)

How it is used: Whether we believe in God or not, we have to believe in an **omniscient**, omnipresent and omnipotent power who runs this world.

My link:

ORACULAR prophetic, relating to divine advice (adj)

How it is used: The warnings of the saint about the drying up of the river due to unplanned development proved to be quite **oracular**.

My link:

PRETERNATURAL beyond normal or natural (n)

How it is used: The disappearance of numerous ships and airplanes at the Bermuda Triangle is still considered to be one of the most **preternatural** occurrences.

My link:

PROFANE not respectful of religious practice, treat with irreverence (adj)

How it is used: It is considered **profane** to not follow the ordained practices during certain parts of the year in many religions.

My link:

PORTEND foretell (v)

How it is used: The soothsayer was scared to **portend** the king's impending death, lest he might get angry and throw him into the dungeon.

My link:

PROSELYTIZE convert from one belief, opinion, or religion to another (v)

How it is used: Even when people convert from one faith to another by their own free will, there is always this doubt if they have been by any chance **proselytized**.

My link:

PURGATORY a state or place of suffering or spiritual atonement (n)

How it is used: In classical Greek plays the hero or protagonist always went through a stage of **purgatory** towards the end.

My link:

QUINTESSENCE most perfect or intrinsic aspect (n)

How it is used: Having a pure heart is the **quintessence** of being a real human.

My link:

REVERENT Showing respect (adj)

How it is used: If we can be **reverent** towards the resources we use and try to give back to Nature, our woes would be over.

My link:

SANCTIMONIOUS to make a show of being morally superior (adj)

How it is used: It is not necessary to be **sanctimonious** in order to appear deeply religious or spiritual.

My link:

SCEPTICAL doubtful (adj)

How it is used: Sarah Lee was **sceptical** about the theory which the scientists propounded to explain the occurrence of crop circles in her neighbouring farms.

My link:

TEMPORAL relating to worldly affairs (adj)

How it is used: In the famous poem 'Ozymandias' by P.B. Shelley, the king is reminded of how **temporal** his powers are, when he sees the fallen statue.

My link:

TENETS a principle or belief (n)

How it is used: The tenets of any religion or faith lie in a common philosophy of goodness, kindness and tolerance.

My link:

TRANSIENT temporary, momentary (adj)

How it is used: During our young age we do not realise how transient beauty and youth are.

My link:

UBIQUITOUS being everywhere (adj)

How it is used: Certain phrases and words are so **ubiquitous** that they can be found in every language in some way or the others.

My link:

VENERATE regard with great respect (v)

How it is used: In this materialistic age, not to venerate money as the ultimate God, is a great virtue in itself.

My link:

ZEALOT	a strict, fanatical follower of a religion (n)
How it is used:	In Mughal dynasty there have been both kinds of rulers, liberal minded like Akbar or **zealots** like Aurangzeb.
My link:	

PRACTICE EXERCISE

Fill in the grid with the correct options in the blank spaces.

WORDS	SYNONYMS	ANTONYMS
1. zealot	fanatic	____________
2. venerate	worship	____________
3. ubiquitious	omnipresent	____________
4. transient	____________	permanent
5. temporal	worldly	____________
6. sceptical	to have doubts	____________
7. sanctimonious	morally superior	____________
8. reverential	worthy of respect	____________
9. quintessence	____________	outwardly
10. purgation	to suffer	____________
11. proselytizing	conversion	____________
12. profane	disrespectful	____________
13. preternatural	paranormal	____________
14. oracular	prophetic	____________
15. omniscient	____________	ignorant
16. occult	supernatural	____________
17. litany	____________	N/A
18. infidel	____________	believer
19. corporeal	____________	ethereal
20. consecrate	purify	____________
21. congregate	____________	disperse
22. celestial	____________	earthly
23. benediction	____________	curse
24. agnostic	____________	devout

N/A: Not applicable

REVIEW EXERCISE–1

Given along with each sentence are three words. Choose the option which fits in best in the given blanks in the sentence.

1. No scientific invention has been able to change the ___________ of life.
(transience, sanctimonious, ubiquitous)

2. Cell phones have become so ___________ that we wonder how we lived without them for so many years.
(oracular, omniscient, ubiquitous)

3. The village people had gathered to listen to the new parishioner's ___________ on the new-age morals.
(litany, profanity, oracle)

4. The monastery was used as a ___________ by the local people. They went and wrote their sins and sought forgiveness.
(purgatory, quintessence, occult)

5. Religions have always vied with one another trying to show one is more ___________ than the other.
(sanctimonius, preternatural, celestial)

6. Several movies have been made on the theme of ___________ phenomena.
(preternatural, celestial, occult)

7. It is surprising that on one hand humans have progressed so much and yet in certain areas ___________ and witchcraft are practised.
(occult, agnosticism, infidelity)

8. There was a time when people in Nepal ___________ their king like God.
(venerated, proselytized, canonized)

9. In those countries, where monarchy is still alive, ____________ powers have been quite restricted and only titular powers have remained.
(temporal, transient, oracular)

10. The ___________ ceremony of the little prince was a grand affair.
(benediction, catechism, corporeal)

11. Why is it that religious intolerance and ___________ is increasing all ever the world?
(zealotry, transience, sanctimony)

12. We are all spending too much time and money on fulfilling our ___________ desires.
(temporal, corporeal, preternatural)

13. The ___________ of vegetarianism is that there is life and feelings in all living beings.
(quintessence, transience, omniscient)

14. Simon was so angry that when he was sacked, he ended up hurling ___________ at his boss.
(profanities, litanies, tenets)

15. Non-violence was the main ___________ of Gandhian philosophy.
(canon, oracle, tenet)

16. On her mother's persuasion, she did attend the hypnotism session but was highly ________ about its efficacy. (sceptical, agnostic, infidel)
17. The new playwright shocked everyone with his __________ views. (iconoclastic, profanity, temporal)
18. The hermit's __________ about the mountain erupting in a volcano came true. (portent, canon, tenet)

REVIEW EXERCISE–2

Now let's see if you are able to recall the words you have learnt in this chapter. A brief definition and the first letter have been given for your help. First one has been done for you.

1. A fanatic	Zealot
2. Relating to body or material	C______________
3. Objects relating to worldly affairs	T______________
4. A church decree	C______________
5. Being morally superior	S______________
6. Purifying with sacred oil	A______________
7. Temporary	T______________
8. Convert one's religion	P______________
9. Intrinsic aspect	Q______________
10. Make sacred	C______________
11. Prophetic	O______________
12. A religious gathering	C______________
13. Possessing all knowledge	O______________
14. Spiritual cleansing	P______________
15. Worthy of respect	R______________
16. Not believing in God	A______________
17. Blessing	B______________
18. Being everywhere	U______________
19. Prophesying doom	A______________
20. Foretell	P______________

Ch: 12 GRAND, ABUNDANT, HUGE —Wow, that's some size

AMPLITUDE breadth, range, magnitude (n)

How it is used: The **amplitude** of the Tsunami warning microphones at the beach was so high that their sound could be heard miles away.

My link:

The **amplitude** of my new stereo system is so high that I can never play it at a high volume.

BURGEONING increasing rapidly (v)

How it is used: **Burgeoning** industries and residential blocks are eating into space needed for farming and agriculture.

My link:

Burgeoning traffic is adding to pollution in my city.

COLOSSAL extremely large (adj)

How it is used: Environmental changes are already leading to **colossal** damage in many countries through forest fires, heavy snowfalls, floods and earthquakes etc.

My link:

COMMODIOUS spacious and roomy (adj)

How it is used: In the club class of the new airbus, the seats are really **commodious**.

My link:

COPIOUS abundant, plentiful (adj)

How it is used: She shed **copious** tears of joy once she heard the news of her husband's safe return from the war.

My link:

CORNUCOPIA abundant supply of good things, a horn (symbol of plentifulness) (n)

How it is used: The soil of the river basin was so fertile that it looked as if the land was blessed with **cornucopia**.

My link:

EMINENT respected, distinguished (adj)

How it is used: All **eminent** personalities of the town gathered for the funeral of the mayor.

My link

GRANDIOSE — impressive, on an ambitious scale (adj)

How it is used: All his **grandiose** plans of holding a massive wedding party for his daughter crashed as she chickened out of the alliance at the last minute.

My link:

LARGESSE — money or gifts given generously (n)

How it is used: When the government keeps giving subsidies and loan waivers to the poor they become used to the **largesse**.

My link:

MAMMOTH — huge (adj)

How it is used: To make the city ready for hosting Olympics in record time proved to be a **mammoth** task for the government.

My link

MEGALOMANIAC — obsessed with power and importance (n)

How it is used: Several world leaders have started in a modest way, but turned into **megalomaniacs** with time and power of might.

My link:

MEGALOPOLIS a very large densely populated city (n)

How it is used: As a city turns into a **megalopolis**, people have to move out to live in suburbs and commute long distances to work.

My link:

MOMENTOUS of great importance (adj)

How it is used: There have been several **momentous** occasions in the history of the world when accords have been signed, and pacts have been inked.

My link:

MULTITUDINOUS consisting of many individuals or elements (adj)

How it is used: There was a **multitudinous** crowd at the International Trade Fair organised in the city for the first time.

My link:

MUNIFICENCE generosity (n)

How it is used: There was one secret donor at the orphanage who was famous for his **munificence** and kindness.

My link:

MYRIAD innumerable, many (n)

How it is used: The **myriad** colours of the autumn leaves lent a unique charm to the park.

My link:

OPULENCE luxury (n)

How it is used: Byzantine Empire established in and around Turkey was known for its **opulence**, and highly decorative and artistic architecture.

My link:

OSTENTATIOUS showy, pretentious display of wealth (adj)

How it is used: With many people joining the exclusive billionaire club, the parties and get-togethers are becoming increasingly **ostentatious**.

My link:

PLENARY absolute, to be attended (adj)

How it is used: The **plenary** session of all members of the Parliament was more of a formality than to conduct any business.

My link:

PLENITUDE condition of being full or complete (n)

How it is used: Thankfully, the weather was good throughout the season and there was a **plenitude** of food and milk at the farm.

My link:

PLETHORA excess of something (n)

How it is used: These days people are spoilt for choice, as there is a **plethora** of options, whether it is for food, clothes or home-utility items.

My link:

PRODIGIOUS remarkably large (adj)

How it is used: Everyone had marvelled at the **prodigious** size and splendour of the Titanic at its maiden trip, not knowing the ill-fate that would befall it.

My link:

PROFUSION plentiful (n)

How it is used: In Rajasthan, as if to counter the arid landscape, there is a **profusion** of colour in the people's costumes.

My link:

PROLIFERATE — increase rapidly in number (v)

How it is used: When law and order are lax, and getting justice is a lengthy procedure, crime of all kinds **proliferates**.

My link

PROPITIOUS — favourable (adj)

How it is used: The weather having been **propitious**, the vineyards showed excellent crop of grapes, ready for making fine wine.

My link:

RAMPANT — growing unchecked (adj)

How it is used: In the absence of effective policing, crime became **rampant** in the township.

My link:

REPLETE — filled, well-supplied (adj)

How it is used: The film-star's house was **replete** with photographs, awards and trophies showing his illustrious film-career.

My link:

SYBARITE lover of luxury (n)

How it is used: Jonathan was such a **sybarite** that he found it difficult to come to terms that his mansion was gone, and so was the bank balance and fan following.

My link:

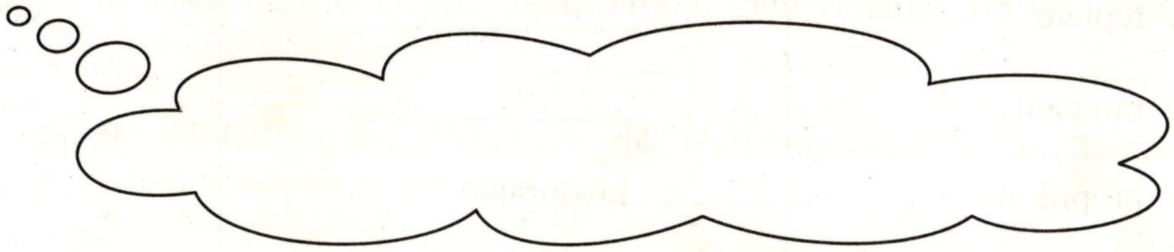

PRACTICE EXERCISE

Fill in the grid with the correct options in the blank spaces.

WORDS	SYNONYMS	ANTONYMS
1. replete	____________	empty
2. rampant	____________	scarce
3. propitious	favourable	____________
4. proliferate	____________	reduce
5. profusion	____________	scarcity
6. prodigious	enormous	____________
7. plethora	____________	shortage
8. plenitude	____________	deficiency
9. plenary	____________	incomplete
10. ostentatious	showy	____________
11. opulence	____________	poverty
12. myriad	____________	singular
13. multitudinous	of many kinds	____________
14. munificence	____________	stinginess
15. momentous	____________	unimportant
16. megalopolis	huge city	____________
17. megalomania	grand plans	____________
18. mammoth	____________	puny
19. largesse	generosity	____________
20. grandiose	impressive	____________
21. eminent	____________	lowly

WORDS	SYNONYMS	ANTONYMS
22. copious	____________	little, less
23. commodious	roomy	____________
24. colossal	huge	____________
25. burgeoning	____________	diminishing
26. amplitude	intensity	____________

REVIEW EXERCISE–1

Find words from the box which mean the same as words given in the list.

proliferating, myriad, profusion, opulence, prodigious, mammoth, munificence

1. colossal M____________
2. burgeoning P____________
3. multitudinous M____________
4. largesse M____________
5. commodious P____________
6. ostentatious O____________
7. plethora P____________

REVIEW EXERCISE–2

Given in front of each word is an option which could either be a synonym or an antonym or none. Choose the right option and put an S or A or N for each of the above given choices. First one has been done for you.

	Word	Option	
1.	amplitude	magnitude	S
2.	burgeoning	diminishing	
3.	eminent	bright	
4.	commodious	room	
5.	cornucopia	horn of plenty	
6.	copious	plentiful	
7.	mammoth	gigantic	
8.	largesse	large	
9.	grandiose	grand	
10.	momentous	important	
11.	myriad	singular	
12.	munificence	magnificence	
13.	plenary	absolute	
14.	prodigious	prodigy	
15.	rampant	dampener	

Ch: 13

HAPPINESS & CONTENTMENT —Smile and the world smiles with you

ALACRITY cheerful readiness (n)

How it is used: Diane agreed to fund the charity ball, and even met the young organisers with such **alacrity** that they were impressed with her commitment.

My link: When our college principal approved the Fest plan, each student of the Cultural Wing got down to work with great **alacrity**.

BEATITUDE supreme blessedness (n)

How it is used: The monks in the monastery up in the Himalayas had an expression of **beatitude** on their faces, it was difficult to say, however if it was the pure mountain air, or peace of solitude.

My link: My grandmother fulfilled each duty with an expression of **beatitude**, and was so active even at the age of ninety.

BLITHE cheerfully indifferent (adj)

How it is used: The children of the Kindergarten school had a **blithe** attitude to life, though for how long they would remain like this, was to be seen.

My link:

BUOYANT cheerful and optimistic, able to keep afloat (adj)

How it is used: Every sailor has to love the sea and sail with a **buoyant** attitude, both literally and symbolically.

My link:

CHORTLE laugh in a hearty, gleeful way (v)

How it is used: Every time someone cracked a joke in the group, howsoever silly it was, Mr. Grant **chortled** with delight.

My link:

DELECTATION pleasure and delight (n)

How it is used: The news of the smashing victory of the college Rugby team at Inter-university tournament was received by the students with much **delectation**.

My link:

DROLL amusing in a strange way (n)

How it is used: The fool in Shakespeare's play was meant to introduce the element of **droll**, at the same time, speaking very wise words about life.

My link:

EBULLIENCE having lot of excitement (n)

How it is used: Little Jane was full of **ebullience** at the thought of going to Disneyland.

My link:

ECSTASY overwhelming feeling of happiness (n)

How it is used: When Becky heard she had been selected for the scholarship at Harward, she was filled with **ecstasy**.

My link:

EFFERVESCENCE enthusiastic (n)

How it is used: The **effervescence** of the young captain brought a certain, youthfulness and urgency to the team's appearance and performance.

My link:

ELATION extreme happiness (n)

How it is used: **Elation** swept through the hearts of several spectators to see their favourite horse winning the race.

My link:

ELYSIAN relating to paradise, blissful (adj)

How it is used: Having got an opportunity to visit the Carribbean islands for a work-cum holiday trip was an **elysian** occasion for Elisa.

My link:

ENTHRAL capture the fascinated attention (v)

How it is used: The audience was **enthralled** at the ballet-dance performance of differently-abled children.

My link:

EUPHORIA feeling of intense happiness (n)

How it is used: When Daisy was told about her pregnancy, her **euphoria** could not last long because being a haemophiliac she was told to take excessive care.

My link:

EXHILIRATING cause to feel very happy or animated (v)

How it is used: Jogging on the beach, dipping feet in the soft sand, with water lapping now and then was very **exhilirating** and refreshing.

My link:

EXUBERANT

lively and cheerful (adj)

How it is used:

During her pregnancy, Madgie looked radiant with an **exuberant** sprint in her step.

My link:

EXULTATION

show or feel triumphant elation (n)

How it is used:

There was a lot of **exultation** in the Smith household when their first member reached college-level and also won a scholarship to New York University.

My link:

FACETIOUS

using inappropriate humour (adj)

How it is used:

Just when the valedictory speech was about to begin, somebody from the audience cracked a very loud **facetious** joke about Mrs. Jenning's dress-sense.

My link:

FELICITY

complete happiness (n)

How it is used:

Deanne wanted to leave her miserable past behind in this city and start a new chapter with a new partner in a new place with complete **felicity** and peace of mind.

My link:

FEISTY spirited and exuberant (adj)

How it is used: The whole family comprised of members each more **feisty** and open-hearted than the other.

My link:

FERVID intensely enthusiastic (adj)

How it is used: Nobody in the town could disregard the children's **fervid** pleas to stop using polythene bags.

My link:

GAIETY state or quality of being light-hearted and cheerful (n)

How it is used: **Gaiety** and festivities marked the three day carnival celebrations in the little town, which came alive with tourists teeming everywhere.

My link:

GRATIFICATION giving pleasure or satisfaction (n)

How it is used: There has been a persistent debate on what is more important: **gratification** of senses or contentment of soul?

My link:

HILARIOUS extremely funny or merry (adj)

How it is used: When the new teacher kept getting mixed up with the two twins it turned into quite a **hilarious** situation.

My link:

JOCULAR fond of joking (adj)

How it is used: Nathan's uncle was a **jocular** ninety-year old man who kept going for his walks till his last day and almost laughed his way to the grave.

My link:

JOVIAL cheerful and friendly (adj)

How it is used: A man in the park, Dan noticed, was quite a **jovial** company, and always had several people crowding around him, laughing and having a good time.

My link:

JUBILIANT happy and triumphant (adj)

How it is used: The most run-down team of the group which was no one's favourite was **jubiliant** at its surprisingly excellent performance and subsequent victory.

My link:

LEVITY treatment of serious matter with humour and lack of respect (n)

How it is used: The whole matter of human rights of the children orphaned by internal strife in countries of Africa was handled with such **levity** that it lost its meaning.

My link:

LUDICROUS absurd, ridiculous (adj)

How it is used: The play was on the whims and sensibilities of the flashy rich people and very appropriately showed actors dressed in **ludicrous** designer clothes.

My link:

RAMBUNCTIOUS uncontrollably exuberant (adj)

How it is used: The country cousin was **rambunctious** from the moment he landed at the New York city because his dream of seeing a big city was coming true.

My link:

RAPTURE feeling of intense pleasure, joy (n)

How it is used: The magic show was so amazing that the audience watched in complete silence and sat with a feeling of **rapture**.

My link:

RAVISHING delightful (adj)

How it is used: The fashion-show by the new designers was not only **ravishing** but also like a breath of fresh air.

My link:

REVELRY lively, noisy festivity (n)

How it is used: They were such a huge Greek family that Sanya's wedding was a week long affair, marked with tables full of food and drinks, songs, dance and **revelry**.

My link:

RHAPSODY enthusiastic expression of feeling (n)

How it is used: The whole class of tiny-tots broke into a **rhapsody** of nursery-rhymes Miss Marples had taught them, during the school inspection.

My link:

SERENDIPITY occurrence of events by chance in a happy way (n)

How it is used: It was complete **serendipity** that Bosco was saving money for a vacation in Hawaii, and suddenly won two free tickets for the same in a lottery.

My link:

SMIRK	smile in a smug, silly way (v)
How it is used:	Joanna felt that she may be a little slow to understand her boss's instructions but there was no need for him to **smirk** and make her further nervous.
My link:	

PRACTICE EXERCISE

Fill in the grid with the correct options in the blank spaces.

WORDS	SYNONYMS	ANTONYMS
1. smirk	smug smile	___________
2. serendipity	luck by chance	___________
3. rhapsody	___________	sorrowful silence
4. revelry	festivity	___________
5. ravishing	delightful	___________
6. rapture	delight	___________
7. rambunctious	happy-go-lucky	___________
8. ludicrous	funny	___________
9. levity	___________	respectful
10. jubiliant	victorious	___________
11. jovial	___________	sorrowful
12. jocular	___________	sad
13. hilarious	comical	___________
14. gratification	___________	disgruntlement
15. gaiety	___________	cheerless
16. fervid	ardent	___________
17. felicity	___________	unhappiness
18. feisty	exuberant	___________
19. facetious	___________	appropriate humour
20. exuberant	lively	___________
21. exultation	sense of victory	___________
22. exhilirating	___________	enervating
23. euphoria	intense happiness	___________

WORDS	SYNONYMS	ANTONYMS
24. enthral	please	____________
25. elysian	____________	hellish
26. elation	happiness	____________
27. effervescence	____________	unenthusiastic
28. ecstasy	____________	despair
29. ebullience	excitement	____________
30. droll	amusing	____________
31. delectation	delight	____________
32. chortle	laugh heartily	____________
33. buoyant	____________	depressed & sinking
34. blithe	____________	worried
35. beatitude	bliss	____________
36. alacrity	____________	unwillingness

REVIEW EXERCISE–1

Choose the word which fits in best in the given blank in each sentence.

smirked, levity, exhilirating, buoyant, blithe, elation, serendipity, delectation, alacrity, hilarious, chortled, ebullient, enthralled, beatitude, revelry

1. The little ballet dancers ___________ the audience with their fluid movements and nimble footedness.
2. Night-long ___________ drained Jenny's spirits completely.
3. Work done with ___________ and dedication speaks for itself.
4. The last year's winners were ___________with the thought that they were the best and would win again.
5. Seeing packets of food and relief material arriving by plane, the flood-victims were filled with ___________.
6. The way the urbane Phoebe ___________ at Betty's rustic simplicity gave the seven-graders much to talk about.
7. The act of the stand-up comedian was so funny that the audience ___________ and guffawed with delight.
8. The ___________ carefreeness of pastoral times is no longer to be felt in these modern times of gadgets and technology.
9. Having met his life-partner at a vacation in Monte Carlo was complete ___________ for Rupert.
10. That the ship was ___________ even after a fierce storm was because of the guts of the captain and his crew.
11. Being in Nature's company at the Hawaaian island filled Mr. Grosnor's heart with ___________.
12. A good shower and drink was truly ___________ after a hard day's work for Mr. Holmes.
13. The children at the middle-school put up such a ___________ costume drama that parents doubled with laughter.
14. To hear that the prisoners of war were being released after ten years of waiting, gave a lot of ___________ to their family members.
15. Just because the departed man was a leader of opposition, the ruling party had no reason to treat the occasion with such ___________ .

REVIEW EXERCISE–2

Given below are a set of words which mean more or less the same. Given in a box are qualities under which these words can be grouped. Put the right quality against each set.

(A) extreme happiness (B) enthusiastic excitement (C) blissful (D) merriment (E) inappropriate and strange humour (F) delight (G) victorious happiness (H) funny and humorous

1. ecstasy, elation, felicity, euphoria ______________
2. rhapsody, exhiliration, ebullience, effervescence ______________
3. ludicrous, levity, facetious, droll ______________
4. jovial, jocular, rambunctious ______________
5. blithesome, serendipity, elysian, beatitude ______________
6. feisty, fervid, revelry, gaiety ______________
7. delectation, rapture, ravish, enthral ______________
8. buoyant, exultant, jubiliant ______________

Ch: 14 HEALTH, FITNESS & MEDICINE —Your health is in your hands

ANOREXIA emotional disorder where losing weight becomes an obsession (n)

How it is used: Recently there has been lot of protest against fashion world's obsession with reed-thin models who may be suffering from **anorexia**.

My link:

I think my teenage sister suffers from **anorexia**, as she hardly eats anything.

ATROPHY wasting away of body tissue or organ/decline in vigour (v)

How it is used: After recovering from a mild paralytic stroke the old man was advised to take to mild exercises to prevent **atrophy** from setting in.

My link:

When my grand father fractured his hip bone and was confined to bed, we feared he would suffer from **atrophy**.

CONTAGIOUS infectious, likely to spread and affect others (adj)

How it is used: The sprightliness and chirpiness of the children's new governess in the baron's house was **contagious** enough to make everyone in the house feel happier and better.

My link:

EMOLLIENT softening or soothing, calming (adj)

How it is used: Her soothing words had an effect of an **emollient** on the war-ravaged orphans huddled in one of the cellars of the broken houses.

My link:

ENDEMIC prevailing in a certain area or group (e.g., a disease) native of an area (adj)

How it is used: Certain kinds of genetic mutation is **endemic** to people living in areas exposed to nuclear radiation.

My link:

EPILEPTIC suffering from nervous disorder and having convulsions (adj)

How it is used: Her **epileptic** seizures became worse after her parents passed away in an air-plane crash.

My link:

INFIRMITY physical or mental weakness (n)

How it is used: It was not clear whether it was the effect of the disease or her lack of enthusiasm in getting better, which was responsible for her **infirmity**.

My link:

MALAISE — a general feeling of discomfort (n)

How it is used: Somehow, people felt a vague sense of **malaise** in the rail coach, not realising that it had been sprayed with nerve gas.

My link:

MYOPIC — short-sighted, lacking foresight or vision (adj)

How it is used: The government's decision to introduce a dedicated lane for luxury buses on the already crowded road turned out to be a very **myopic** move, as it led to accidents, traffic jams, and total confusion.

My link:

NAUSEATE — to make sick, fill with disgust (v)

How it is used: The horrid sight of the decomposing body filled with maggots **nauseated** even the most toughened cops sent to unearth the stench in the apartment.

My link:

OPIATE — derived from opium, inducing a false sense of contentment (n)

How it is used: The doctors did not realise that the cough syrup she was being given, would become like an **opiate**, to be used by her whenever she felt disturbed at the death of her husband.

My link:

PALLIATIVE relieving pain or alleviating a problem without dealing with the cause (adj)

How it is used: Though the pain-killers did not cure her arthritis it did work as a **palliative** and made movement less painful.

My link:

PANACEA a remedy for all diseases or difficulties (n)

How it is used: If only there was a **panacea** for the environmental problems that are looming large over the world, things would be so much easier.

My link:

PANDEMIC a disease which spreads over a large part of the world (adj)

How it is used: Medical experts at one time feared that the AIDS epidemic if not checked in time, would turn into a **pandemic**.

My link:

PESTILENCE a fatal epidemic disease (n)

How it is used: After the floods, the most dreaded fear was the outbreak of **pestilence** in the village.

My link:

PHLEGMATIC — unemotional and stolidly calm (adj)

How it is used: Though people with a **phlegmatic** disposition, appear cold and aloof, they can handle situations of crisis better than hyper active creatures.

My link:

PHOBIA — extreme irrational fear of something (n)

How it is used: Her **phobia** of heights turned her into a nervous wreck, limiting her life so badly that she had to give up her work and sit at home.

My link:

PLACEBO — a substance having no medicinal effect but used for psychological benefit (n)

How it is used: To some patients who suffer from imaginary diseases, doctors prescribe **placebos**, to quell their symptoms and interestingly, they seem to get better also.

My link:

PROGNOSIS — forecast about the likely course of a disease (n)

How it is used: The doctor's **prognosis** that the patient would begin recovering on his own, as the giddiness was caused by a self-limiting virus proved to be correct.

My link:

PROPHYLACTIC intended to prevent a disease (adj)

How it is used: As soon as the flood waters receded, the government took all **prophylactic** measures, to prevent outbreak of gastroenteritis, yet cases surmounted creating an epidemic like situation.

My link:

PROTUBERANCE bulging, protruding (n)

How it is used: Though initially the **protuberance** on his leg looked like a harmless cyst, but soon turned gangrenous and painful.

My link:

PSYCHOSIS a mental disorder which makes one lose touch with reality (n)

How it is used: After the accident, the fear **psychosis** in Mary Jane became so strong, that she shuddered at the sound of any screeching brakes.

My link:

PSYCHOSOMATIC relating to interaction of mind and body (adj)

How it is used: Certain diseases can't be treated at the physiological level, they have to be treated more holistically at the **psychosomatic** level.

My link:

PULMONARY relating to lungs (adj)

How it is used: Doctors discovered that smoking had destroyed his **pulmonary** veins without any scope of their recovery.

My link:

QUARANTINE isolation of a person, place or animal for fear of spreading infection (n)

How it is used: As soon as the news of bird flu spread, the consignment of chicken arriving from neighbouring countries was **quarantined**.

My link:

RECUPERATE to recover from illness, regain (v)

How it is used: She was sent to the hospice so that her frail body could **recuperate** from the prolonged chemotherapy she had undergone for her cancer.

My link:

RESUSCITATE revive from unconsciousness, make active again (v)

How it is used: It was not easy to **resuscitate** the girl because she had been drowned in the pool for quite some time.

My link

SALUBRIOUS health giving, pleasant (adj)

How it is used: In the earlier days it was common for doctors in the U.K. to prescribe tuberculosis patients to move to more **salubrious** environs of places like Sicily and Naples.

My link:

SALUTARY beneficial, health-giving (adj)

How it is used: The cool relaxed atmosphere of the Spa-cum-resort had a **salutary** effect on her, as she lay recovering from a bitter and broken marriage.

My link:

THERAPEUTIC having a good effect on body and mind (adj)

How it is used: Hot sulphur springs are supposed to contain **therapeutic** properties particularly for skin diseases.

My link:

PRACTICE EXERCISE

Fill in the grid with the correct options in the blank spaces.

WORDS	SYNONYMS	ANTONYMS
1. therapeutic	healing	____________
2. salutary	____________	harmful
3. salubrious	____________	unpleasant
4. resuscitate	revive	____________
5. recuperate	recover	____________
6. quarantine	____________	allowed to pass through
7. psychomatic	____________	physiological
8. psychosis	mental disorder	____________
9. protuberance	protruding	____________
10. prophylactic	preventive	____________
11. phobia	irrational fear	____________
12. phlegmatic	unemotional, calm	____________
13. panacea	a universal remedy	____________
14. palliative	pain relieving	____________
15. opiate	____________	stimulant
16. nauseate	disgust	____________
17. myopic	____________	far-sighted
18. malaise	discomfort	____________
19. infirmity	____________	strength
20. epileptic	having nervous disorder	____________
21. endemic	disease of an area	____________
22. emollient	soothing	____________
23. contagious	infectious	____________
24. atrophy	loss of vitality	____________
25. anorexia	____________	obesity

REVIEW EXERCISE–1

Given below are sentences which have blanks. Choose the word which fits in best in the given blank from the given options.

infirmity, epileptic, phobia, contagious, therapeutic, myopic, anorexic, nauseated, atrophy, salutary, quarantined, malaise, panacea, recuperate, emollient, endemic, opiates

1. There are several professions where the employees can't afford to have a _________ vision.
2. The _________ effect of the pure air of mountains cannot be debated upon.
3. In the tribal village they applied an _________ made from some local herbs on the injured traveller.
4. Certain diseases which were earlier _________ to certain areas are now becoming globalised because of increasing international travel and mixing of people.
5. Isn't it strange that on one hand the young are suffering from obesity and on the other hand some others are so conscious that they become _________ .
6. Some people are able to fight _________ induced by illness by sheer will power.
7. The scientific world is now opening to the _________ value of many kitchen products, herbs and 'grand mothers' prescriptions made with turmeric, basil, neem etc.
8. The doctors could do nothing to cure Henry of the _________ he had of wearing neck ties in case he suffocated.
9. Though Samantha was fine as long as she was in the asylum, under the supervision of doctors, but soon enough after returning home she started getting her _________ fits again.
10. When she sat in the aeroplane for the first time, she started feeling _________ as soon as it took off.
11. After an injury, limiting a patient to bed-rest can lead to _________ of back muscles and restrict his movement further.
12. Using _________ can make people dependent on them for life.
13. What would you say is the biggest_________ of modern society: lack of moral values, increasing consumerism or an i-me-myself attitude.
14. Yoga and meditation are being now considered as a _________ to many modern lifestyle diseases.
15. It has been medically proven that yawning can be _________.
16. The space-ship was _________ after its return to the earth in case it may be carrying germs from the other planets' soil.
17. She was given all kinds of treatment to help her _________ from the shock of her children's murder.

REVIEW EXERCISE–2

CROSSWORD

Given below is a crossword based on the words just learnt. Based on the clues given fill in the right word.

CLUES

Across

1. I am very scared of cockroaches, I think I am _____________.
2. When I have a headache, I use strong coffee as an _____________.
3. When we get injured and do not use a limb for a long time we might feel ___________ setting in.
4. I suffered from _____________ in the extremely crowded train compartment.
5. My mother applied an _____________ on my grazed knees and elbows when I was a child.
6. Unemployment is the biggest _____________ of poor countries.
7. With age everyone's eyesight seems to turn _____________ .

Down

1. I wish there was a _____________ for all our problems.
2. I think my greatest _____________ is my indecisiveness.
3. Everybody agrees that laughter is _____________ .
4. Lot of people think that homeopathic medicines work only as a _____________ .
5. Is terrorism _____________ to only certain countries, or is it spread wider than we think?
6. In the old world several villages were wiped out due to one _____________ or the other.

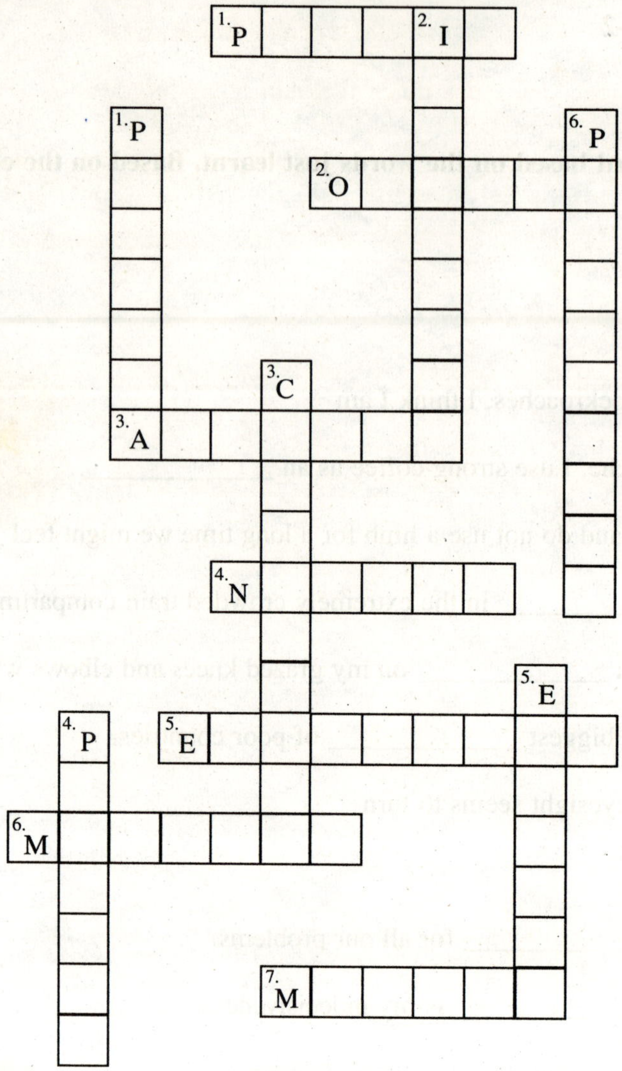

Ch. 15 HISTORY —Past keeps coming back

AEONS indefinite, long period of time (n)

How it is used: Sometimes events from the past appear as if they had just happened yesterday, while on other occasions, it appears that they had happened **aeons** ago.

My link:

Now that I have moved to another city, it appears I haven't met my friends for **aeons**.

ANNALS record of events (n)

How it is used: Sufferings of mankind at the hands of tyrannic rulers over the centuries are recorded in the **annals** of History.

My link:

The year I won the chess championship, my name got recorded in the **annals** of school history.

ANTEDILUVIAN extremely ancient, ridiculously old-fashioned (adj)

How it is used: It is strange how what was fashionable and modern in the grandparents time starts looking almost **antediluvian** to the new generation.

My link:

ANTIQUITIES old fashioned, outdated (n)

How it is used: Sometimes, what is considered as an **antiquity** is resurrected and revived to start modern trends.

My link:

BOURGEOIS of middle class, having materialist values (adj)

How it is used: It would not be inappropriate to say that the modern world of consumerism is creating an even bigger **bourgeois** population.

My link:

CHRONICLE a detailed written account of important events (n) record (v)

How it is used: He tried to **chronicle** a family tree by using the family records in the house library, and pictures kept in the albums.

My link:

COMMEMORATE honour the memory of as a mark of respect (v)

How it is used: The Gateway of India was built as a triumphal arch to **commemorate** the visit of King George V and Queen Mary.

My link:

MAUSOLEUM a stately building, housing a tomb (n)

How it is used: Taj Mahal is the most beautiful and exquisite of all the **mausoleums** in the world.

My link:

OBSOLESCENCE becoming obsolete (n)

How it is used: With the advent of digital technology gadgets based on analog technology have faded into **obsolescence**.

My link:

PAPYRUS early paper made from stem of a water plant (n)

How it is used: Before paper was invented, people of ancient civilizations were using **papyrus** to write on, or parchment, tablets and other tree leaves or bark to document various events and facts.

My link:

PHILISTINE a person hostile to culture and arts (n)

How it is used: Sometimes all kinds of cultural advancement and literary freedom is curbed when power falls into the hands of **philistines**.

My link:

PRIMORDIAL primitive, from the beginning of time (adj)

How it is used: Many native tribes in the interiors of Africa, still live in the same **primordial** ways.

My link:

PROGENITOR an ancestor or parent, originator of something (n)

How it is used: Most of the African slaves brought by whites in the early 18th century are **progenitors** of the present day Afro-Americans.

My link:

PROLETARIAT working class people (used with reference to Marxism) (adj)

How it is used: Though communism had sprung up to tackle the problems of **proletariats** in Russia, it is not sure whether it was really successful in doing so.

My link:

PROVENANCE place of origin, earliest known history of something (n)

How it is used: Archaeologists, paleontologists and historians are all interested in knowing about the **provenance** of different things.

My link:

RELIC surviving remains of history (n)

How it is used: **Relics** of ancient civilizations can be found in several famous museums.

My link:

REMNANT small remaining quantity (n)

How it is used: The **remnants** and ruins discovered at the excavation site were a witness that a thriving civilization, rich in culture, had once existed there.

My link:

RETROSPECTIVE looking back on past events (adj)

How it is used: A **retrospective** of Alfred Hitchcock's films was held on the occasion of World Cinema Summit at Hollywood.

My link:

RUNIC written or set in ancient alphabet, mysterious (adj)

How it is used: Lot of historical evidence from several ancient civilizations is still lying unread because it is in some **runic** alphabet and script.

My link:

SCION	a descendant of a notable family (n)
How it is used:	Though he was the **scion** of the biggest industrial house of the country, his simplicity was truly admirable.
My link:	
SECESSION	act of withdrawing formally from a political or religious organisation (n)
How it is used:	When India got its independence, besides the problem of partition, it had several states demanding **secession** from the Republic.
My link:	
SEDITION	conduct or speech inciting rebellion (n)
How it is used:	The fiery speech given by the revolutionary leader did not lead to open bloodshed but did amount to **sedition**.
My link:	
SEPULCHRE	a small room or monument in which someone is buried (n)
How it is used:	The prodigal son of the nobleman was buried in a **sepulchre** in the family graveyard.
My link:	

SPARTAN showing indifference to comfort or luxury (adj)

How it is used: During India's freedom struggle many nationalist leaders shunned British patronisation and luxurious lifestyle to lead a **spartan** life which could inspire the young generation.

My link:

SUPERANNUATED too old to be effective or useful (adj)

How it is used: It is sad how as the world is increasingly becoming more and more technologically advanced, work is being done by the younger lot and the old are being **superannuated**.

My link:

UNRAVEL unwind, investigate, solve (v)

How it is used: With the excavation of the ancient Roman site, lot of mysteries about the civilization have been **unravelled**.

My link:

USURP take illegally or by force (v)

How it is used: There have been several instances in history of a power hungry prince killing his own brethren to **usurp** the throne.

My link:

VESTIGES trace of something, the smallest amount, remains (n)

How it is used: **Vestiges** of merry-making by the poachers could be seen in the jungle from the blood-stains, bones, hair and a still burning fire left behind by them.

My link:

PRACTICE EXERCISE

Fill in the grid with the correct options in the blank spaces.

WORDS	SYNONYMS	ANTONYMS
1. vestiges	traces	____________
2. usurp	____________	give away
3. unravel	disentangle	____________
4. superannuated	____________	effective
5. spartan	____________	indulgent
6. sedition	____________	subordination
7. secession	____________	inclusion
8. scion	____________	noble ascendant
9. runic	____________	N/A
10. retrospective	____________	futuristic
11. remnant	remainder	____________
12. relic	remains	____________
13. provenance	origin	____________
14. proletariat	working class	____________
15. primordial	primitive	____________
16. progenitor	____________	descendant
17. philistine	____________	cultured
18. obsolescence	obsolete	____________
19. commemorate	____________	forget
20. chronicle	written account	____________
21. bourgeois	middle class	____________
22. antiquities	outdated	____________
23. antediluvian	____________	modern
24. annals	record of events	____________
25. aeons	long period of time	____________

N/A: Not applicable

REVIEW EXERCISE–1

Choose the answer that is most nearly opposite in meaning to the word and fill in the options in the circle given. First one has been done for you.

Answer

1. retrospective
   (A) pondering (B) perspective (C) looking back at the past (D) looking at future — Answer: (D)
2. philistine
   (A) cultured and broad-minded (B) philandering (C) modern (D) ancient (E) restrictive — Answer: ( )
3. commemorate
   (A) forgive (B) forget (C) honour (D) memorise (E) sympathise — Answer: ( )
4. antiquities
   (A) old-fashioned (B) modern (C) outdated (D) historical (E) antique — Answer: ( )
5. bourgeois
   (A) of middle-class (B) materialistic (C) ancient (D) elite (E) of working-class — Answer: ( )
6. chronicle
   (A) report (B) detailed account (C) events (D) record (E) undocumented — Answer: ( )
7. primordial
   (A) primitive (B) modern (C) ordeal (D) primary (E) antique — Answer: ( )
8. progenitor
   (A) originator (B) ascendent (C) procreator (D) progeny (E) old generation — Answer: ( )

9. obsolescence
   (A) obsolete (B) contingency (C) contemporary
   (D) insolence (E) essence

10. proletarian
   (A) bourgeois (B) nobility (C) working class people
   (D) commoners (E) comrades

11. runic
   (A) mysterious (B) back-biter (C) tresspasser
   (D) simple (E) runaway

12. remnant
   (A) complete whole (B) remainder (C) ruins
   (D) rampant (E) less quantity

13. secede
   (A) withdraw (B) join (C) snatch
   (D) seize (E) accede

14. spartan
   (A) luxurious (B) disciplined (C) stern
   (D) indifferent (E) rigid

15. sedition
   (A) rendition (B) subordination (C) authority
   (D) treason (E) rebellion

16. unravel
   (A) mystify (B) reveal (C) desire
   (D) complicate (E) force

17. usurp
   (A) usual (B) taken illegally (C) give voluntarily
   (D) snatch (C) violence

18. aeons
   (A) annals (B) scions (C) ages
   (D) moments (E) years

REVIEW EXERCISE–2

Given along with each sentence are three words. Choose the option which fits in best in the given blanks in the sentence.

1. The _________ of the ancient civilization are now being re-discovered through new excavations and studies. (annals, remnants, antiquities)
2. Building magnificent _________ was an integral part of Mughal architecture and culture. (mausoleums, provenance, sculptures)
3. His _________ lifestyle could not show that he was a legendary leader of world fame. (proletarian, primordial, spartan)
4. When he arrived on the international political scene very few people knew that he was a _________ of the famous first family of the country. (remnant, scion, chronicle)
5. A glorious ceremony was held to _________ the golden jubilee of the illustrious institution. (commemorate, unravel, superannuate)
6. These days there are newer models and versions of gadgets entering the market so fast that the existing ones are _________ relatively quickly. (superannuated, usurped, seceded)
7. If only local history of a place was as painstakingly _________ as it is of important places, people would be more interested in history. (unravelled, chronicled, commemorated)
8. _________ of several great civilizations can be found in their excavations. (aeons, vestiges, provenance)
9. Tales of glory of ancient civilisations are recorded in the _________ of history. (mausoleum, annals, papyrus)
10. ___________ of technology from day to day is turning earth into a huge dumping ground of e-waste. (obsolescence, remnant, provenance)
11. That archaeologists have risked their lives to _________ the secrets of Egypt's pyramids is remarkable. (unravel, usurp, superannuate)
12. In some democratic countries it is common for the military to stage a coup and _________ power from the elected government. (usurp, commemorate, secede)
13. In a _________ of the functioning of the government it was found that it had not fared too badly. (secession, sedition, retrospective)
14. No creature of _________ times has generated as much interest or scientific research as dinosaurs have. (bourgeois, antediluvian, philistine)
15. Sometimes your own childhood incidents become so faded in your memory they appear to have occurred _________ ago. (aeons, annals, vestiges)

Ch: 16 KNOWLEDGE & WISDOM
—Thinking ways to be a know-it-all

ACUMEN ability to take quick decisions (n)

How it is used: The government had complete faith in his diplomatic **acumen**, and sent him to diffuse the international political mess, which the new foreign affairs minister had put the country into.

My link:

When I left home for the first time I realised how I had to use my **accumen** and take decisions on my own all the time.

ACUITY sharpness of thought, vision or hearing (n)

How it is used: Thanks to all the sophisticated gadgetry and technology are we losing our own **acuity** and becoming totally dependent on these devices?

My link:

Its amazing how my grandmother still uses her **acuity** of vision and manages without glasses.

ADJUDICATE make a formal judgment (v)

How it is used: Everyone was relieved when the matter was **adjudicated** in favour of the complainant even though he had raised the issue against the tobacco baron.

My link:

APPRAISE assess the value of (v)

How it is used: The new boss was not sure how he would **appraise** his team since he did not know them so well as yet.

My link:

APPRISE inform (v)

How it is used: The Governor asked the secretary of state to **apprise** him of the progress of relief measures for the earthquake victims.

My link:

ARBITRATE act as judge, settle a dispute (v)

How it is used: It was important for local council to **arbitrate** the matter between the displaced natives and the builders' lobby to ensure early settlement.

My link:

ASCERTAIN find out for certain (v)

How it is used: It was easy to **ascertain** that the guest lecturer was a well-travelled man and had lots of anecdotes up his sleeve, to narrate to the class.

My link:

ASTUTE wise, having good judgment (adj)

How it is used: An **astute** lawyer that he was, he noticed the subtle gap between the version of witness one and witness two in the murder story that had been beautifully cooked up by the defense side.

My link:

CEREBRAL intellectual, related to brain (adj)

How it is used: Inspite of being born in a family of intellectuals, her knowledge and interest in the **cerebral** discussions held at her home was minimal.

My link:

COGENT clear, logical, convincing (adj)

How it is used: He was awarded full scholarship for Harvard because not only was his academic record brilliant, but also his papers were written in a **cogent** style and were very well presented.

My link:

COGITATE meditate, reflect (v)

How it is used: Except for a few, most board members were of the opinion that the decision should be taken immediately, and there was no need to **cogitate** any further.

My link:

COGNIZANCE — knowledge or awareness (n)

How it is used: It was later revealed that the terrorist attack on the ammunition depot had taken place with full **cognizance** of the exiled military commander.

My link:

CONNOISSEUR — an expert judge in matters of art etc. (n)

How it is used: He was known to be a **connoisseur** of art, with a huge collection of his own, and always in demand to give his opinion on the works of new and emerging artists.

My link:

CONTEMPLATE — think profoundly (v)

How it is used: After he passed out in the conference hall due to overwork and stress, he was forced to **contemplate** the course his life had taken after he had joined his new job.

My link:

DISCERNIBLE — that which can be distinguished or understood (adj)

How it is used: The changes in the weather patterns due to global warming are quite **discernible** now.

My link:

DISCRETION the ability to decide what should be done (n)

How it is used: Generally Samantha exercised a lot of **discretion** with her clients because her job of being a marriage counsellor demanded it of her.

My link:

DILETTANTE an amateur follower of the arts (n)

How it is used: Though she pretended to be an authority on modern genres of painting, a little probing on the part of the media persons revealed she was no more than a **dilettante**.

My link:

DOGMATIC strictly adhering to principles or fixed ideas (adj)

How it is used: Daniel could not realise that his lectures would generally sound very **dogmatic** and theoretical and bored the students.

My link:

ELUCIDATE make clear, explain (v)

How it is used: The research scholar was asked to **elucidate** several controversial topics he had touched upon in his thesis on the morality aspect of genetics.

My link:

EMERITUS having retired but allowed to retain a title as an honour (adj)

How it is used: He was awarded the title of Professor **Emeritus** at the age of ninety which was a record in itself.

My link:

EMPIRICAL based on observation and experience (adj)

How it is used: What made his arguments noteworthy was that they were based on **empirical** evidence and not on mere notions.

My link:

ERUDITE learned, having knowledge (adj)

How it is used: The new Principal at the Law College was an **erudite** man with several years of legal and academic experience behind him.

My link:

FATHOM understand after much thought (v)

How it is used: The child could not **fathom** why the father would become so angry whenever he asked about his mother.

My link:

INTELLIGENTSIA — intellectual and educated group of people (n)

How it is used: The **intelligentsia** of any country has to take interest in the governing of the country to bring valuable changes in the society.

My link:

LAUREATE — a person given an award for outstanding achievement (n)

How it is used: Wordsworth is considered as the poet **laureate** of the Romantic Era of English Literature.

My link:

LUMINARY — a person who inspires or influences others (n)

How it is used: Some universities become a renowned seat of learning over the years, as they have the pride of producing several **luminaries** in different disciplines.

My link:

PENSIVE — engaged in deep thought (adj)

How it is used: He generally remained in a **pensive** and sombre mood, after he was diagnosed with blood cancer.

My link:

PERCEPTIVE having acute insight (adj)

How it is used: The lady boss at the Cola company was liked by her staff because she seemed to be quite **perceptive** and sympathetic towards their personal needs and problems.

My link:

PERUSE read or examine thoroughly (v)

How it is used: It would have been better if Laura had **perused** the fine print of the deal, then she would not have been duped so badly.

My link:

PERSPICACIOUS having a good understanding of things (adj)

How it is used: The new lawyer in the famous Benson Group of legal experts climbed fast in the eyes of his seniors because of the **perspicacious** analyses he did of difficult cases.

My link:

PERSPICUOUS something which is clearly expressed and easily understood (adj)

How it is used: Since people knew her frank nature they did not mind her **perspicuous** comments and candid confessions.

My link:

PRECOCIOUS having developed certain abilities at an earlier age than usual (adj)

How it is used: When Peter began to speak within a few months of his birth, his parents thought that he was a **precocious** child.

My link:

PRECOGNITION foreknowledge (n)

How it is used: **Precognition** has always mystified scientists and featured as a desirable faculty in many science-fiction movies.

My link:

PROCTOR an officer at a university (having disciplinary function) (n)

How it is used: When certain students were found indulging in writing graffiti on the main hall's walls they were summoned by the **Proctor.**

My link:

PROPOSITION statement expressing judgment or opinion (n)

How it is used: The famous pharmaceutical company got into a buy-out contract with a smaller, lesser known company because of the attractive **proposition** it made in front of the board members.

My link:

PROPOUND put forward (an idea or theory) for consideration (v)

How it is used: The concept of zero was first **propounded** in India.

My link:

PRUDENT wise, careful (adj)

How it is used: When everyone expected her to be more **prudent** about her future relationships she went and got married to a complete jerk.

My link:

RUMINATE think deeply, chew over and over (chew cud like cows) (v)

How it is used: After retirement suddenly he was left with so much time that he began to **ruminate** about how he could most gainfully spend his day and energy.

My link:

SAGACIOUS having good judgment and insight (adj)

How it is used: The grand old uncle in the family was dreaded but still obeyed and respected by the huge family of four generations because of his **sagacious** attitude and vision.

My link:

PRACTICE EXERCISE

Fill in the grid with the correct options in the blank spaces.

WORDS	SYNONYMS	ANTONYMS
1. sagacious	perceptive	________
2. ruminate	________	act hastily
3. prudent	________	imprudent
4. propound	develop	________
5. proposition	________	negation, cancellation
6. prodigy	with exceptional intelligence	________
7. precognition	________	after-thought
8. precocious	________	late-bloomer
9. peruse	________	read casually
10. perspicuous	________	create confusion
11. perspicacious	having a good understanding	________
12. perceptive	having insight	________
13. pensive	________	thoughtless
14. luminary	________	ordinary person
15. intelligentsia	________	working class
16. fathom	________	not understand
17. erudite	learned	________
18. empirical	________	without any experience
19. elucidate	________	befuddle
20. dogmatic	sticking to principles	________
21. discretion	________	imprudence
22. discernible	________	indistinguishable
23. dilettante	________	expert

WORDS	SYNONYMS	ANTONYMS
24. contemplate	think deeply	________
25. connoisseur	________	amateur
26. cognizance	________	unacceptance
27. cogitate	think over	________
28. cogent	________	unconvincing
29. cerebral	pertaining to brain	________
30. astute	________	foolish
31. ascertain	________	to doubt
32. arbitrate	settle a dispute	________
33. apprise	________	keep in dark
34. appraise	assess	________
35. adjudicate	________	not judge
36. acumen	mental sharpness	________
37. acuity	________	dullness

REVIEW EXERCISE–1

Given along with each sentence are three words. Choose the option which fits best in the given blanks in the sentence.

1. An ____________ study is being done to find the effects of mobile radiation on human brain cells. (empirical, cerebral, dogmatic)
2. His ____________ prevented the company from forging an absolutely foolish deal with the great retail giant. (erudition, sagacity, proposition)
3. The company director thought that Susan was taking a hasty decision in quitting the job and asked her to ____________ over her decision before he accepted her resignation. (ruminate, discern, arbitrate)
4. The government spent a lot of time in ____________ the merits of the new subsidies on agriculture for cotton farmers. (elucidating, discretion, cogitating)
5. Though he was new to the famous Brett and Lee firm of solicitors and was handling his first case yet his arguments were ____________ enough to match those of any seasoned lawyer. (cogent, discretion, precognition)
6. The consumer forum wanted to ____________ the reason for the delay in compensation to the client, from the side of the medical agency. (discern, ascertain, arbitrate)
7. Is it true that ____________ and age go together or some people can be foolish even in old age? (prudence, discretion, arbitration)
8. The floor manager wanted to know if the store owner had been ____________ of the severe staff shortage. (appraised, propounded apprised)
9. Certain mysteries of nature are still ____________ in spite of lot of research and analysis. (cogent, unfathomable, propositioned)
10. A ____________ change has come about in people's value system and code of conduct in this modern 'I, me, myself' times. (discernible, dogmatic, cognizance)
11. When analysed, the prodigy's ____________ capabilities invoked great admiration from the school council. (empirical, cerebral, appraisal)
12. The ____________ of the fresh reporters at the new TV Station was impressive. (cognizance, perspicacity, perception)
13. It required lot of professional ____________ to negotiate with the striking employees and come up with a win-win solution for the union leaders and the management. (acumen, dogma, arbitration)
14. The captain decided to use his ____________ and rest the very capable but injured batsman and use the thirteenth player instead. (elucidation, appraisal, discretion)
15. The new governor belied his age and his looks to prove that he was well-informed in the matters of governance and ____________ in his decisions. (empirical, pensive, astute)

16. It was an interesting _____________, given by Senator McGill to waive off the taxes of the population suffering due to the Hurricane Katrina but the opposition thought it was economically unviable. (proposition, discretion, perception)

17. If humans had the ability of _____________, as sometimes shown in Science Fiction movies would the world be a better place to live, with no crime at all? (precognition, perception, proposition)

18. When the old man saw his friends dying one after the other, he became distraught and _____________, spending more and more time in his study. (contemplating, pensive, prudent)

19. Several _____________ of the town were called at the Diamond Jubilee celebration of the University. (intelligentsia, luminaries, prodigies)

20. It took Mark's parents some time to understand that his early passion for music was a sign of his being a _____________ at playing the piano which he finally mastered at the age of ten. (prodigy, cogent, erudite)

21. Martha was a rather _____________ child, she could understand philosophy and theology at the age when other children were still reading bed-time stories. (perspicuous, precocious, perspicacious)

22. What was remarkable about Hubert was that he was equally capable of light-hearted banter as he was of _____________ and scholarly discussion. (prudence, erudition, precognition)

23. When the early scientific theories were being _____________ no one had thought that they would have such far reaching influences and would become the base for much sophisticated technology and development. (cogitated, discerned, propounded)

24. In the new talk show the anchor had a style of raising some controversial topics and expecting the guest celebrity to _____________ them. (elucidate, ascertain, arbitrate)

25. It is true that modern man is so engrossed in his day to day existence that time to _____________ or ponder over the richness of life is just not there. (contemplate, discern, perceive)

26. All along while the management was trying to strike a deal with the labour union, it was in _____________ of the owners' plan to announce a lock-out. (contemplation, cognizance, perception)

27. When it was time for the annual _____________, the company decided to retrench several of the employees on the basis of their performance. (appraisal, arbitration, adjudication)

28. Certain situations in life make you so panicky that you need _____________ of all senses to survive. (perusal, prudence, acuity)

REVIEW EXERCISE–2

A. There are groups of 4 words given. In each group there are three synonyms and one odd word. Find which is the odd word out and write its option in the circle given. First one has been done for you.

	Answer
(i) (A) cogitate (B) elucidate (C) ruminate (D) contemplate	(B)
(ii) (A) fathom (B) discern (C) ascertain (D) adjudicate	◯
(iii) (A) astute (B) sagacious (C) pensive (D) erudite	◯
(iv) (A) precocity (B) discretion (C) prudence (D) perspicacity	◯

B. Given below are definitions of words or their opposites. Also given in the box are the words which have to be written in front of their correct options. Choose the right word. First one has been done for you.

pensive, cerebral, luminary, dilettante, perspicuous, apprise precognition, adjudicate, propound, ruminate, appraisal, cogent, emeritus, acumen, intelligentsia, perceptive, arbitrate, connoisseur

(i) ability to decide fast acumen

(ii) illogical ____________

(iii) intellectual ____________

(iv) an expert in some matters ____________

(v) an amateur or who dabbles in art ____________

(vi) somebody who has retired but is still honoured ____________

(vii) a person who is learned and inspires others ____________

(viii) the intellectual or educated class ____________

(ix) engaged in deep thought ____________

(x) not clear or easily understood ____________

(xi) intuitive ____________

(xii) after thought ____________

(xiii) make a formal judgment ____________

(xiv) act as a judge to settle disputes ____________

(xv) put forward a theory ____________

(xvi) keep in dark, not inform ____________

(xvii) process of assessing the value of something ____________

(xviii) think over and over again ____________

(xix) a person who receives an award ____________

(xx) a person who looks after discipline at university ____________

Ch: 17

LITERATURE
—Who hasn't read any?

ADAGE — wise saying, proverb (n)

How it is used: There is lot of merit in the **adage** about honesty being the best policy.

My link: I wonder if today's generation believes in the **adage** 'Old is Gold' any longer.

ADDENDUM — an extra item added at the end of a book or text (n)

How it is used: The plot was so obscure that it could not be understood till people had read the **addendum**.

My link: My brother is so lost, that his sentences can only be understood once he speaks the **addendum**.

ALLEGORY — a story, poem, picture with a hidden meaning (n)

How it is used: It was clear that the play was an **allegory** of Paradise lost, a modern adaptation of Satan's life.

My link:

ALLUSION indirect or implicit reference (n)

How it is used: Henry's remarks towards Billy Bob's erratic behaviour had a strong **allusion** to his even more wayward past.

My link:

ANALOGY comparison between two things in order to explain something (n)

How it is used: The dentist gave the **analogy** of little monsters to explain the work of bacteria in the children's teeth at the preparatory school session.

My link:

ANNOTATE add notes (to a text or diagram) in order to explain (v)

How it is used: J.R.R. Tolkein liberally **annotated** the text of Lord of the Rings to make reading simpler for children.

My link:

ANTHOLOGY collection of music, poetry or art (n)

How it is used: The **anthology** of the art displays in the museum had been put together by the curator who was an artist himself.

My link:

APHORISM — a statement which contains general truth (n)

How it is used: His speeches were always peppered with **aphorisms** which made them quite a hit with the audience.

My link:

APROPOS — (a) with reference to (prep)
(b) to the point, appropriate (adj)

How it is used: (a) **Apropos** the young tennis player's achievement, the overwhelming turn out of the crowd was but natural.

(b) A placatory comment coming from the President was **apropos** to the rapidly deteriorating situation between the two state governments.

My link:

ARCHAIC — old or old fashioned (n)

How it is used: Its strange how in one's own life time certain mannerisms, and traditions become **archaic**, and new ones take their place.

My link:

AXIOM — an accepted statement (n)

How it is used: In a democracy it is **axiomatic** that the power of selection or rejection of a government rests with the people.

My link:

BANAL unoriginal, commonplace (adj)

How it is used: What started as an intelligent effort at humour in the play, soon turned out to be a **banal** attempt at making people laugh at silly situations.

My link:

CATHARSIS process of releasing pent-up emotions (n)

How it is used: Crying openly by men in these days is considered to be more of a **cathartic** process than a sign of weakness.

My link:

CLICHÈ overused phrase or opinion (n)

How it is used: These days if someone talks about principles like "slow and steady wins the race", it sounds very **clichèd** to the young generation.

My link:

COROLLARY direct consequence or result (n)

How it is used: When disaster strikes, people's lives are so shattered that in many cases psychological problems are considered to be a natural **corollary.**

My link:

DENOUEMENT — the final part of a play, film or narrative (n)

How it is used: Though the **denouement** of the play was very predictable, the treatment of the plot was very sensitively handled.

My link:

DIRGE — a mournful song/lament for the dead (n)

How it is used: Since the baron was quite a popular man, all townspeople began to weep, as soon as the **dirge** was played at the funeral.

My link:

ELEGY — a mournful poem (n)

How it is used: Sir Elton John's famous song 'Candle in the Wind' has become almost like an **elegy** for Princess Diana.

My link:

EPIGRAM — a short witty poem, or saying (n)

How it is used: John Donne, the famous metaphysical poet wrote most of his poetry in **epigrammatic** style.

My link:

EULOGY speech or piece of writing which praises someone highly (n)

How it is used: Its customary to **eulogise** people after their death, howsoever fallible or human they may have been.

My link:

EUPHEMISM polite word for something harsh or unpleasant (n)

How it is used: A lot can be conveyed through **euphemism** instead of being rude or harsh.

My link:

GENRE a style of art or literature (n)

How it is used: Science-fiction and fantasy writing are the most selling **genres** of literature these days.

My link:

HERCULEAN requiring great strength or effort (adj)

(derived from Hercules, Greek hero known for his strength.)

How it is used: Clearing the site of the twin towers of the World Trade Centre of the debris was a **herculean** task, both in terms of physical and emotional effort.

My link:

HYPERBOLE exaggeration (n)

How it is used: I find modern man's claim of his life becoming simpler because of technological advancement, a complete **hyperbole**. Aren't we busier, less healthier and more stressed out?

My link:

IRONIC happening in opposite way to what is expected (adj)

How it is used: It was **ironic** that Mr. James should do the same things that he told his son not to do, now that he was dead and gone.

My link:

MAXIM a short statement expressing a general truth (n)

How it is used: Children's stories and folk tales in almost all cultures are based on some common **maxims**.

My link:

MISNOMER wrong use of name or term (n)

How it is used: Calling today's several politicians by the name of leaders would be quite a **misnomer**.

My link:

PARABLE — a simple story with a moral or spiritual lesson (n)

How it is used: We have all heard and read many **parables** in childhood, yet how many do we remember or practise in life?

My link:

PASTORAL — relating to countryside, as in farming, grazing etc. (adj)

How it is used: Very soon people are going to get tired of urban life and would want to go back to the simple, idyllic **pastoral** life of the country folks.

My link:

PATHOS — a quality that evokes pity or sadness (n)

How it is used: The subtle element of **pathos** in the story of Rebecca keeps the readers hooked till the end.

My link:

PLAGIARISM — taking off someone's idea, and pretend its one own (n)

How it is used: Many young designers thrive on **plagiarism**, which they shamelessly call inspiration.

My link:

POLEMIC — a strong verbal or written attack (n)

How it is used: During the elections, each party indulges in **polemics** of every kind, even leading to mud-slinging at times.

My link:

PROTÈGÈ — a person guided by an older or influential person (n)

How it is used: Sometimes **protègès** have outdone their masters in the same skill that they were trained in.

My link:

PSEUDONYM — a fictitious name used by an author. (n)

How it is used: There has always been a trend for authors to use **pseudonyms** for penning their works.

My link:

SOBRIQUET — nickname (n)

How it is used: Some actors become so famous by their **sobriquets** that people don't even know their real names.

My link:

SOLILOQUY speaking aloud to oneself like in a play (n)

How it is used: Hamlet's **soliloquies** are famous as they give an insight into his insecurities and doubts.

My link:

SPOONERISM error in speech, getting mixed up in letters (n)

How it is used: Many tongue-twisters can lead to accidental **spoonerisms**.

My link:

STYGIAN dark, deathly, derived from Styx, underworld river in Greek mythology (adj)

How it is used: There was a **stygian** darkness in the castle's dungeons, reminding people of various prisoners who may have died there, waiting for their freedom.

My link:

SUBLIME of great excellence or grandeur (adj)

How it is used: The whole world has been in awe of the **sublime** musical talent of Pandit Ravi Shankar.

My link:

UTOPIA an imaginary perfect place or situation (n)

How it is used: To some extent Ayn Rand talks about a **utopian** land in her novel. Atlas Shrugged, where all the characters of her book go to live.

My link:

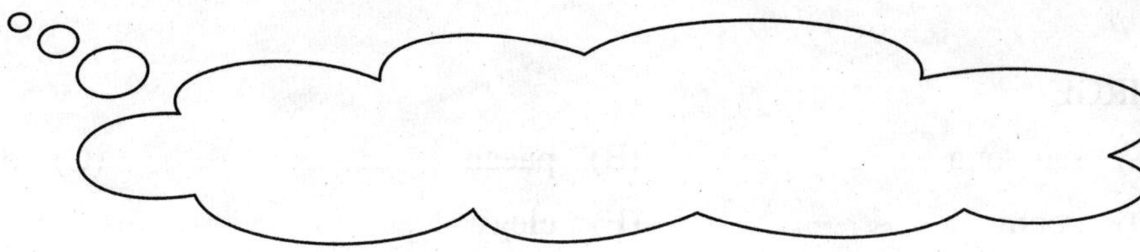

PRACTICE EXERCISE

Choose the option that is opposite in meaning to the words given and write the answer in the circles given.

Answers

1. DIRGE
   (A) sad song (B) paean (C) drudgery
   (D) poem (E) elegy ◯

2. EUPHEMISM
   (A) unpleasant way of putting things (B) false show (C) exaggeration
   (D) emphasis (E) polite form of expression ◯

3. SOLILOQUY
   (A) oblique (B) dialogue (C) monologue
   (D) solitude (E) solicit ◯

4. EULOGY
   (A) praise (B) theology (C) theory
   (D) criticism (E) prodigy ◯

5. BANAL
   (A) bane (B) boon (C) vain
   (D) drudgery (E) exalted ◯

6. PATHOS
   (A) evoking pity (B) state of no feeling (C) bathos
   (D) empathy (E) truth ◯

7. ALLUSION
   (A) referring implicitly (B) illusion (C) delusion
   (D) direct reference (E) hallucination ◯

8. PARABLE
   (A) amoral (B) moralistic story (C) payable
   (D) ability (E) comparable ◯

9. APHORISM
   (A) a lie (B) axiom (C) maxim
   (D) parable (E) schism ◯

10. ARCHAIC
(A) arching (B) modern (C) curved
(D) obsolete (E) aching

11. COROLLARY
(A) cause (B) result (C) consequence
(D) corolla (E) reference

12. CLICHÈ
(A) commonplace (B) repetitive (C) overused term
(D) norm (E) unique phrase

13. HERCULEAN
(A) effortless (B) epicurean (C) caesarean
(D) majestic (E) difficult

14. PROTEGÈ
(A) patron (B) student (C) guide
(D) self-made person (E) disciple

15. PLAGIARIZE
(A) copy (B) make original and unique (C) scandalize
(D) suffocate (E) make it worse

16. PASTORAL
(A) rural (B) romantic (C) related to church
(D) urban (E) beautiful

17. SUBLIME
(A) commonplace (B) condense (C) oblige
(D) evaporate (E) define

18. ADAGE
(A) wise saying (B) foolish statement (C) average
(D) extension (E) of age

19. HYPERBOLE
(A) understatement (B) exaggeration (C) hyperactive
(D) desire (E) bold

20. IRONY
(A) ironing out (B) felony (C) stony
(D) twist of fate (E) mean the same as

REVIEW EXERCISE–1

Match the definitions with the words.

Column A	Column B
1. overused phrase	(a) dirge
2. short, witty saying	(b) euphemism
3. a simple story with a moral	(c) soliloquy
4. a meaningful saying	(d) eulogy
5. purging or cleansing	(e) elegy
6. lamenting music	(f) banal
7. an accompaniment	(g) pathos
8. an accepted truth	(h) addendum
9. strong verbal attack	(i) allusion
10. getting mixed up in letters	(j) allegory
11. a style of literature	(k) parable
12. mild way of saying something unpleasant	(l) utopia
13. of rural life	(m) analogy
14. an ideal place or situation	(n) annotate
15. praise	(o) anthology
16. requiring great effort	(p) aphorism
17. talking to oneself	(q) apropos
18. a story with symbolic meaning	(r) archaic
19. final outcome of a literary work	(s) axiom
20. a saying or a proverb	(t) maxim
21. similarity, creating a parallel	(u) catharsis
22. an addition to text	(v) clichè
23. nickname	(w) corollary
24. steal another's ideas and make them one's own	(x) epigram
25. collection of literary works	(y) herculean

26. writing under a false name	(z) polemic
27. a wrong name	(a^1) protègè
28. quality of pity	(b^1) sobriquet
29. noble and lofty	(c^1) spoonerism
30. old fashioned, obsolete	(d^1) genre
31. appropriate and to the point	(e^1) plagiarism
32. a person with protection and support	(f^1) pastoral
33. indirect reference	(g^1) pseudonym
34. make explanatory comments	(h^1) misnomer
35. commonplace	(i^1) sublime
36. mournful poem	(j^1) denouement
37. exaggerated way of saying	(k^1) hyperbole
38. contrary to expectation	(l^1) irony

REVIEW EXERCISE–2

Choose the word which fits in best in the given blank in each sentence.

denouement, sublimity, pseudonym, clichèd, addendum, allusions, anthology, archaic, herculean, plagiarism, genres, catharsis, soliloquies, apropos, pastoral, allegory, analogies, corollary, protegè, pathos, hyperbole.

1. It was a one man show where the dramatist depicted the travails of modern man through beautifully rendered _________.

2. The report in the newspaper had missed on details which had to be quickly inserted through an _________.

3. In the speech of the company CEO, on the occasion of the award-giving ceremony, there were _________ to the brilliant record of certain employees.

4. Police's quick handling of the tense situation was _________to the fraying sentiments of the huge mob that had gathered there.

5. An _________ of Shakespeare's complete works including his plays and sonnets has hit the market.

6. Lot of people are worried that the way letter-writing has become a lost art, similarly the art of writing by hand is becoming _______.

7. Once his family deserted him he went through a ________ and decided to change his ways.

8. Is it true that honesty and truthfulness have become ________ concepts in the modern world rather than being the virtues they were.

9. After the landslide, pulling out people from under the mud and debris required ________ efforts.

10. Most of the readers do not know that Mark Twain, is a ________ and not his real name.

11. Romantic poets tried to counter the artificiality of the life of nobility by talking about the simplicity of ________ life.

12. Who decides what is ________, and what is inspiration from old films or classics.

13. There are several writers, trying to break moulds and writing in new ________ of literature.

14. Works of great authors have stood the test of time because of the ________ and universality of the emotions depicted in them.

15. George Orwell's Animal Farm can be considered as an ________ on Europe's situation after World War II.

16. Sometimes it appears as if Nature's fury and waywardness is a ________ to man's selfish plundering of the natural resources.

17. Ralph was the famous designer Emenillo's ________ till he decided to part ways and start his own label.

18. Greek classical plays worked a lot around evoking ________ among its readers and then leading to the ________.

19. Children can be taught a lot about life through the ________ of their games and stories.

20. That the sky is falling was not actually a ________ for Chicken Little.

Ch: 18 LOVE & FRIENDSHIP —All is fair in love

AFFABLE good natured, sociable (adj)

How it is used: Our first landlord was an **affable** man who adopted us when we were newly-weds almost like his children.

My link: My grandfather is an **affable** man and the whole colony's children crowd around him for stories and games he plays with them.

AFFILIATION association, to be connected with an organisation (n)

How it is used: Ever since he became the students' union President, his **affiliation** with politically minded people grew.

My link: My **affiliation** is with the social unrest group, not with their political leanings.

AFFINITY natural liking, closeness (n)

How it is used: She has a great **affinity** for any animal, she sees, in distress.

My link:

AMENABLE open to suggestion (adj)

How it is used: The good thing about the new teacher was that she was **amenable** to certain suggestions given by her students and certain leniencies they demanded from her time to time.

My link:

AMIABLE friendly, pleasant (adj)

How it is used: Since the two countries were in a cold war situation, it was not expected that the talks would take place in an **amiable** environment.

My link

AMICABLE friendly, without discord (adj)

How it is used: They decided to end their seven year long relationship and part from each other in an **amicable** manner.

My link:

AMITY friendly relations (n)

How it is used: If the whole world lived with **amity** and goodwill, it would be such a peaceful place.

My link:

AMOROUS showing or feeling sexual desire or love (adj)

How it is used: The **amorous** advances of the lion towards the lioness at the zoo gave the hope of a new generation being born.

My link:

BETROTHED engaged to be married (v)

How it is used: They had been **betrothed** to be soon married till the cruel hand of fate snatched him away from her.

My link:

BEWITCHED enchanted, delighted (v)

How it is used: The knight was **bewitched** by the beauty of the princess.

My link:

BON-HOMIE good-natured friendliness (n)

How it is used: The good food and **bon-homie** at the fashion designer's party was famous in the fashion-fraternity.

My link:

CAMARADERIE mutual trust and friendship (n)

How it is used: Children who don't know each other till a day before, develop **camaraderie** with each other when staying under one roof in the boarding school.

My link:

CONCORDANCE in agreement, or harmony (n)

How it is used: In **concordance** with his wishes, his entire property was given away to the charitable hospital.

My link:

CONFIDANTE a person in whom someone confides (n)

How it is used: It was not clear whether Jane was just Mr. Kubrick's **confidante** or much more.

My link:

CONVIVIAL friendly, lively, enjoyable (adj)

How it is used: The best thing about the dinner party at Jenny's place was that there was a **convivial** atmosphere, all trying to enjoy in their own way.

My link:

ENAMOUR — filled with love or admiration (v)

How it is used: The young model was so **enamoured** of the glamour and glitz of the fashion-world that she couldn't see the sweat and grind behind it.

My link:

ENDEARMENT — love or affection (n)

How it is used: They were so engrossed in whispering words of **endearment** in each other's ears that they did not notice the ground shaking beneath them due to the earthquake.

My link:

ENRAPTURE — give intense pleasure (v)

How it is used: The enthralling performance by the prodigy musicians left the audience completely **enraptured**.

My link:

FIDELITY — loyalty to a person or cause (n)

How it is used: No one could question Mr. Jackson's **fidelity** to the organisation, he had been there ever since company had been founded by the senior Mr. Welles.

My link:

FRATERNIZE be on friendly terms (v)

How it is used: The first year student was quick to make friends and **fraternize** even with seniors easily.

My link:

GENIAL friendly, cheerful (adj)

How it is used: It was difficult to believe that the actor who had been most **genial** and pleasant to the journalists, would suddenly clam up when questions were asked about his recent divorce.

My link:

INCLINATION natural tendency or liking (n)

How it is used: She had shown no **inclination** to take to the family business up till now.

My link:

INFATUATION short-lived passion (n)

How it is used: Who hasn't gone through crushes in school, or felt an **infatuation** towards classmates or teachers?

My link:

LIAISON

communication between people or organisation (n)

How it is used:

It was difficult to believe that all along while negotiations were on between the merger of two companies, their top manager was in **liaison** with a rival company, leaking out all secrets to them.

My link:

PARAMOUR

lover, illicit partner of a married person (n)

How it is used:

The man was found to be murdered in a most brutal way and the police suspected the hand of his **paramour** with whom he was living after having left his wife and family.

My link:

PLIANT

flexible, easily swayed (n)

How it is used:

She was **pliant** as long as her interest was not sabotaged.

My link:

PROCLIVITY

inclination, predisposition (n)

How it is used:

She had a **proclivity** to get into trouble howsoever miles away she might be from it.

My link:

UXORIOUS showing great fondness for one's wife (adj)

How it is used: His overt display of affection, his complete obedience and **uxorious** attitude towards his wife made him the butt of many jokes.

My link:

PRACTICE EXERCISE

Fill in the grid with the correct options in the blank spaces.

WORDS	SYNONYMS	ANTONYMS
1. uxorious	loyal to wife	____________
2. proclivity	inclination	____________
3. pliant	____________	rigid
4. liaison	come together, communicate	____________
5. infatuation	attraction	____________
6. inclination	____________	lack of desire
7. genial	____________	unfriendly
8. fraternity	brotherhood	____________
9. fidelity	____________	disloyalty
10. enrapture	please	____________
11. endearment	____________	unfeeling
12. enamoured	attracted	____________
13. convivial	friendly, lively	____________
14. confidante	____________	not to be trusted
15. concordance	____________	disagreement
16. camaraderie	trust, friendship	____________
17. bon-homie	____________	hostility
18. bewitched	enchanted	____________
19. amorous	____________	detached
20. amity	friendship	____________
21. amicable	____________	discordant
22. amiable	pleasant	____________
23. amenable	flexible	____________
24. affinity	____________	dislike
25. affiliation	____________	disassociation
26. affable	____________	unsocial

REVIEW EXERCISE–1

Match each word with its definition

Column A	Column B
1. amenable	(a) sociable
2. affable	(b) without discord
3. amity	(c) open to suggestion
4. amicable	(d) affection
5. amiable	(e) engaged
6. amorous	(f) enchanted
7. bewitched	(g) filled with love
8. betrothed	(h) pleasant
9. concordance	(i) pleasant environment
10. bon-homie	(j) harmony
11. camaraderie	(k) friendship
12. endearment	(l) cheerful
13. enamour	(m) mutual trust
14. confidante	(n) brotherhood
15. enrapture	(o) natural liking
16. fraternity	(p) short lived passion, sexual desire
17. genial	(q) communication
18. inclination	(r) easily swayed
19. infatuation	(s) predisposition
20. liaison	(t) fondness for one's wife
21. paramour	(u) intense pleasure
22. pliant	(v) illicit partner
23. proclivity	(w) admiration
24. uxorious	(x) trustworthy
25. convivial	(y) cheerful and friendly

REVIEW EXERCISE–2

Choose the word which fits in best in the given blank in each sentence.

affiliations, amicable, concord, affability, bewitching, pliant, proclivity, amenable, liaisons, geniality, enamoured, infatuation, endearing, camarderie, fraternity, inclination, enraptured, convivial.

1. Her __________ looks was a distraction to many in the neighbourhood.
2. There was a great __________ in the house as long as the grandfather was alive and kept everyone together.
3. Janet's and Morgan's ______ became the talk of the small town within no time.
4. It is becoming difficult for parents to explain their teenage children that what they feel at that age may be just __________ and not true love.
5. The opposition was __________ on the condition that its terms of agreement be met.
6. Her __________ for order and neatness sometimes seemed to be bordering on madness.
7. The __________ of the new team-leader was exceptional and every employee wanted to be in his group.
8. The __________ words of the husband failed to make the wife's anger melt.
9. Sometimes people can be handled better with _______________ rather than rudeness and meanness.
10. So __________ was he of her ravishing beauty that he lost all sensibility and sanity.
11. The entire student __________ stood up against the dean's decision to ban student's union activities in the campus.
12. The parents watched their tiny tots performing with an __________ silence.
13. When they kept postponing the date of their engagement, Shaila realised that he had no __________ of making the commitment.
14. In order to be successful in the working arena one has to be __________ to what others in the team might be saying.
15. After the acrimonious fight in the court between Kate and Daniel, it was not likely that they would ever be on __________ terms again.
16. It was appreciable that the two warring companies had reached the negotiating table and some __________ was about to take place.
17. Though she was new to the job but the __________ atmosphere helped her to settle fast.
18. My __________ with my previous organisation helped me in understanding the new set up better.

Ch: 19 MONEY, MONEY, MONEY
—Its a rich man's world

ACCRUE increasing amounts of money over time (v)

How it is used: Why should man only worry about **accruing** his monetary wealth, why not think about the profit to be gained from good deeds?

My link:

Once I borrowed a lot of money from my friends and my debts **accrued**.

AUGMENT to increase (something) by adding to it (v)

How it is used: The overseas students have to **augment** their stipend income by doing odd jobs to meet their study and living expenses.

My link:

I decided to **augment** the supply of water by adding a booster pump to the main line.

DEFRAY provide expenses or cost (for something) (v)

How it is used: She was obliged when the company decided to **defray** the cost of her journey back home due to her mother's sickness.

My link:

ESCALATION increase rapidly (n)

How it is used: The moment it was announced that Olympic Games would be held in the city, property prices of the area **escalated** overnight.

My link:

EXORBITANT unreasonably high (price or charge) (n)

How it is used: The price of the cottage at the beach-front was **exorbitant** and yet had many takers for the exquisite view it presented of the sea-side.

My link:

FILCH steal, pilfer (v)

How it is used: Who hasn't **filched** cookies from their mother's larder, or fruits from the neighbour's garden in their childhood?

My link:

FRUGAL economical with money or food (adj)

How it is used: After her husband's death, her **frugal** lifestyle kept her in good stead, and helped bring her two children up rather comfortably.

My link:

GRATIS free of charge (adv)

How it is used: If the government gives too many subsidies and freebies to people, they only get encouraged to live on **gratis**.

My link:

GRATUITY money paid to employee at the end of a period of employment (n)

How it is used: Richard did not make any provisions for his post-retirement life because he was hopeful of living comfortably off his **gratuity** and other funds.

My link:

IMPECUNIOUS having little or no money (adj)

How it is used: He claimed to be an **impecunious** man when it came to sharing it with society but spent lavishly on himself.

My link:

INCREMENT increase or addition (n)

How it is used: The new pay commission was not in favour of yearly **increment** in salaries, and wanted to give only a one-time increase.

My link:

INDEMNITY security against loss of financial burden (n)

How it is used: Generally government officials are provided **indemnity** against third party law suits.

My link:

LUCRATIVE profitable (adj)

How it is used: He was himself fond of dreaming big, and sold dreams and ideas to those who would buy and made it into a **lucrative** business.

My link:

MERCANTILE relating to trade or commerce (adj)

How it is used: In this world of trade and commerce, taking up **mercantile** law as a profession seems to be a sensible decision.

My link:

MERCENARY motivated by desire for gain (adj)

How it is used: For years, sophisticated weapons have been sold to terrorists by those **mercenaries** who are only interested in earning money through violence and bloodshed.

My link:

PARSIMONIOUS unwilling to spend, thrifty (adj)

How it is used: Inspite of having a large amount of money, his **parsimonious** habits annoyed his family members.

My link:

PATRIMONY property inherited from one's father or male ancestor (n)

How it is used: Being a sole heir, he became a millionaire overnight after getting **patrimony** from his deceased uncle.

My link:

PECUNIARY relating to money (adj)

How it is used: Traditional arts and crafts are dying because of lack of state support and **pecuniary** benefits in many developing countries.

My link:

PENURY extreme poverty (n)

How it is used: Inspite of several measures to boost the farm-sector, farmers are leading a life of **penury** and starvation.

My link:

PERQUISITE a special privilege enjoyed because of one's position (n)

How it is used: What is intended as a **perquisite** should remain so and not become a part of one's salary or asked as a matter of right.

My link:

PRODIGAL wastefully extravagant (adj)

How it is used: After he had squandered all the family wealth on gambling and betting, the **prodigal** son returned home to seek forgiveness.

My link:

PROFLIGATE wasteful, reckless, immoral (adj)

How it is used: Her friends were **profligate** in all sense of the word: stole money and led an insensitive life, fuelled by drinks, passion and drugs.

My link:

RETRENCH reduce expenditure to cut costs (v)

How it is used: **Retrenchment** of workers and down-grading of companies is the first sign of an economy going into recession.

My link:

SQUANDER waste something in a reckless manner (v)

How it is used: Whatever the father had earned through his hard work all his life, the son **squandered** all that on women and wine within no time.

My link:

USURY practice of lending money at high rate of interest (n)

How it is used: In Shakespeare's play 'The Merchant of Venice', Antonio hates Shylock because according to him Shylock indulges in **usury**.

My link:

PRACTICE EXERCISE

Fill in the grid with the correct options in the blank spaces.

WORDS	SYNONYMS	ANTONYMS
1. usury	lend at a very high rate	__________
2. squander	__________	save
3. retrench	cut down expenditure	__________
4. profligate	wasteful and immoral	__________
5. prodigal	wasteful	__________
6. perquisite	gain above salary	__________
7. penury	poverty	__________
8. pecuniary	related with money	__________
9. patrimony	__________	N/A
10. parsimonious	__________	extravagant
11. mercenary	for monetary gain	__________
12. mercantile	__________	N/A
13. lucrative	__________	loss-making
14. indemnity	security	__________
15. increment	increase	__________
16. impecunious	__________	rich, affluent
17. gratuity	__________	N/A
18. gratis	__________	costing money
19. frugal	economical	__________
20. filch	steal	__________
21. exorbitant	__________	moderate
22. escalation	__________	reduction
23. defray	pay the cost	__________
24. augment	increase	__________
25. accrue	__________	take away by subtraction

N/A: Not applicable

REVIEW EXERCISE–1

Choose the word which fits in best in the given blank in each sentence.

perquisites, exorbitant, accrued, gratis, mercantile pecuniary, lucrative, indemnity, filching, penury, squandering, retrenched, prodigal, gratuity, frugality, augment, escalating, impecunious, defray, parsimonious, usury

1. The hostile conditions at the border were only ___________ the conflict and a war seemed likely.
2. The ravaging floods reduced so many people to ___________ as their homes and belongings were swept away.
3. The government was forced to take many ___________ measures in order to control inflationary disturbances.
4. Instead of ___________ away all the inheritance, he was advised to invest it in property and company shares.
5. ___________ to employees only make sense if they are largely tax-free.
6. His ___________ lifestyle attracted the attention of several banks he had taken loans from.
7. Due to a slow-down in the economy, employees salaries and perks in several companies had to be ___________.
8. Churning out self-help and motivational books in this era of quick solutions seems to be a ___________ business these days.
9. She tried to ___________ her income from her teaching job at the village, by taking private tuitions in the evening.
10. One day the store keeper caught one of the helping staff _________ money from the cash-box.
11. ___________ has been the mantra of all great men be it M.K. Gandhi, Abraham Lincoln or Martin Luther King.
12. The wayward son of the millionaire was set free on bail for drug possession against an ___________ of several thousand dollars.
13. What the local people thought was some kind of dirt was sold at an ___________ amount as it contained traces of radio-active material.
14. Her debts ___________ even as she struggled to continue her late father's staggering business.
15. Advertisers know that the offers of discounts and freebies which are ___________ with products, are a big temptation for consumers.

16. Employees in the hospitality and beauty sector sometimes earn as much as salaries through ___________ received from clients and customers.

17. The ___________ grand-father was reluctant to distribute his large wealth amongst his grand-children.

18. Lots of new career opportunities are coming as the world of ___________ and commerce is becoming more global and e-enabled.

19. We can't deny that many young recruits come into the army for ___________ reasons and not just for patriotism.

20. The crash in the world share market left him ___________ .

21. The company was ready to ___________ the cost of his sickness provided he put in extra hours later.

22. In some religions lending money for interest is as good as ___________.

REVIEW EXERCISE–2

CROSSWORD

Given below is a crossword based on the words just learnt. On the basis of the clues given, fill in the right word.

Across

1. If you stole something from your neighbour's garden it would be called ___________.
2. If you tried to increase the air conditioning at your home you would ___________ global warming.
3. If you tipped the waiter at the restaurant he would be thankful for the ___________.
4. If you ask an arms supplier why he does this work, it would be for purely ___________ reasons.
5. Would you agree if I said poetry emerges out of ___________.
6. Remember, parents always advised not to ___________ away all your pocket money but save something for a rainy day.
7. When you were younger you got everything ___________, now you have to earn for it.
8. When you realise you are spending too much on your petrol-bill, you would be forced to introduce some ___________ measures.

Down

1. You had thought of some innovative business ideas which looked to be very ___________ but did not turn out to be so in practice.
2. You thought you could ___________ your pocket money by working in a departmental store in the evenings.
3. When you want to cut costs, you ___________ the expenditures.
4. If I gave you a monthly raise for your good work, it would be called an ___________.
5. If you got lot of money from your great grand father's estate, it would be a huge ___________.
6. If you do good deeds to others, their blessings would ___________.

1. F
1. L
2. E
2. A
3.
3. R
4. I
4. M
6. A
5. P
6. S
7. G
8. P

Ch:20 NEGATIVE EMOTIONS —Never did anybody good

ACERBIC forthright and sharp tone (adj)

How it is used: In the world of journalism, one has to be very careful in wording criticism, because very **acerbic** write-ups can cost you your job.

My link:

My uncle's way of talking was very **acerbic** and hurting.

ACRIMONY bitterness or ill feeling (n)

How it is used: It is strange how often some people start their relationship on notes of love and commitment, and yet very soon end in blame-game and **acrimony**.

My link:

My neighbours had an **acrimonious** fight for the custody of their daughter during the divorce proceedings.

APPALLING horrifying, displeasing (v)

How it is used: Her mean behaviour of calling everybody names at her stepfather's funeral was **appalling**.

My link:

BRUSQUE — abrupt in speech or manner (adj)

How it is used: People stopped minding her comments when they realised that she was by nature **brusque**, and did not mean any harm to anyone.

My link:

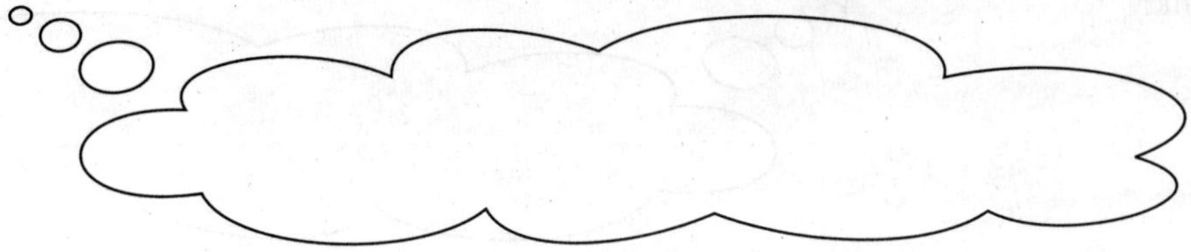

CAUSTIC — marked by incisive sarcasm (adj)

How it is used: The starlet's remarks against other actresses were **caustic** and in very poor taste.

My link:

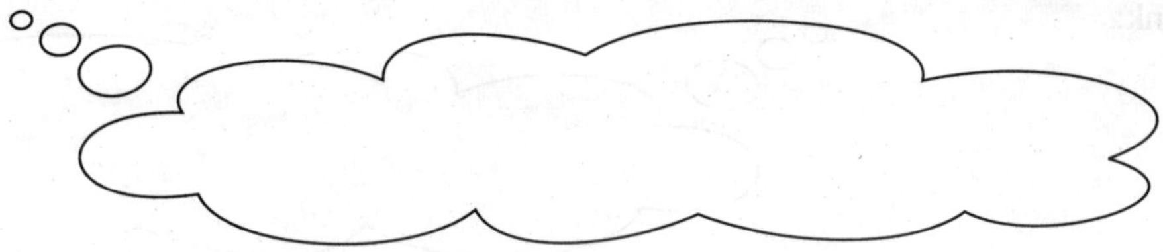

CONTENTIOUS — to cause disagreement or controversy (adj)

How it is used: All over the world, several islands are disputed and it is **contentious** as to which country they belong to.

My link:

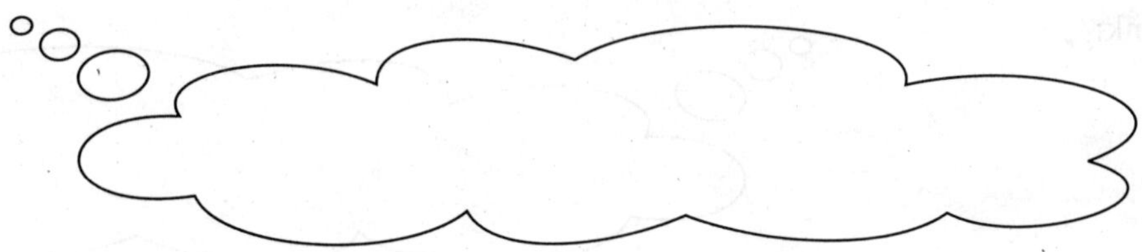

CONTUMACIOUS — stubborn, disobedient (adj)

How it is used: In spite of the government declaring strikes unlawful, the **contumacious** employees stopped work and came out on the streets demanding better wages.

My link:

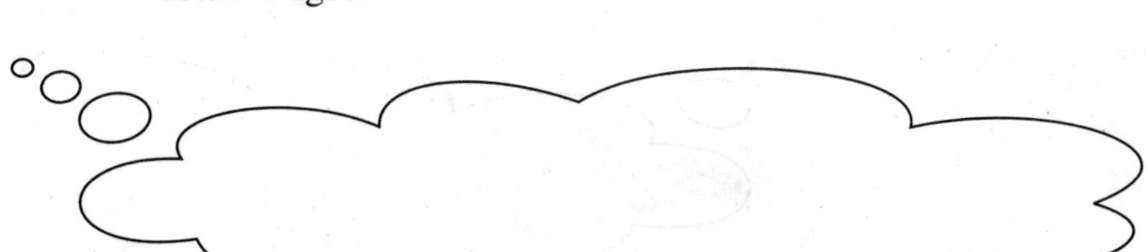

DELETERIOUS	causing harm or damage (adj)
How it is used:	In spite of knowing that smoking was extremely **deleterious** to his failing health, he continued to smoke almost a pack a day.
My link:	
DEPLORABLE	shockingly bad (adj)
How it is used:	After her new found success, the model behaved snobbishly with everyone at the party, and people found her behaviour **deplorable**.
My link:	
DESPICABLE	deserving hatred and contempt (adj)
How it is used:	Always treating her help as if she was dirt showed a very **despicable** behaviour on her part.
My link:	
DESULTORY	lacking purpose or enthusiasm (adj)
How it is used:	Though Buck left home in a huff, after an altercation with his wife, yet he roamed here and there in a **desultory** manner, waiting for her call.
My link:	

DIATRIBE ironic or satirical criticism (n)

How it is used: Somehow the elections turned into a lot of **diatribe** and mud-slinging between the two presidential candidates.

My link:

DISPARAGE degrade, to depreciate by indirect means (v)

How it is used: Whatever John did, his parents always **disparaged** him in front of others.

My link:

EXACERBATE make something worse (v)

How it is used: He thought his placatory comments would ease the tension but they could not have the desired effect and rather **exacerbated** the situation.

My link:

EXASPERATE irritate intensely (v)

How it is used: Peter was quite **exasperated** to see his son suffer because of his habit of postponing important tasks.

My link:

EXECRATE — feel or express great loathing (v)

How it is used: The estate manager was so ruthless to the slaves that they **execrated** his every word, and helpless to do anything, just wished for God to punish him.

My link:

FLAGRANT — conspicuously wrong, blatant (adj)

How it is used: U.N. tries to intervene in situations where there might be **flagrant** violation of human rights of people of any country.

My link:

FRACTIOUS — easily irritated, difficult to control (adj)

How it is used: After a major bout of sickness the child became **fractious** and whimsical.

My link:

GRIMACE — ugly, twisted expression on face showing pain or disgust (n) or (v)

How it is used: Her friends had by now realised that it was impossible for her to be cheerful, she could only to carry herself with a constant **grimace**.

My link:

INGRATE — an ungrateful person (n)

How it is used: Though the Smiths had brought up the orphan John like he was their own child, he turned out to be quite an **ingrate** and left them alone, to pursue his own lavish lifestyle.

My link:

INSOLENT — rude and disrespectful (adj)

How it is used: Initially the parents did not check his behaviour, and later George grew into quite an **insolent** creature.

My link:

INSOUCIANT — indifferent, unconcerned (adj)

How it is used: Though Jordan did come for the inquest of his first wife's murder, he looked quite unfazed and **insouciant**.

My link:

INVECTIVE — critical or abusive language (n)

How it is used: At the slightest delay, the man started hurling **invectives** at the salesman for not showing him the products in the show case.

My link:

INVIDIOUS unacceptable, arousing ill will or resentment (adj)

How it is used: Nobody in the group paid much attention to her **invidious** remarks, because they knew her envious nature.

My link

IRASCIBLE ill-tempered (adj)

How it is used: The new headmaster was known for his **irascible** temper and not allowing anyone to speak directly to him.

My link:

MORBID abnormal interest in unpleasant things e.g., death or disease (adj)

How it is used: Media's intrusion in people's lives at the time of tragedy or disaster, creates a **morbid** curiosity among the viewers' mind.

My link:

OSTRACIZE exclude from a society or group (v)

How it is used: Since people thought she was a witch and possessed supernatural powers, they **ostracized** her from the village.

My link:

PEJORATIVE expressing contempt or disapproval (adj)

How it is used: In politics people can sink really low and mar their rivals' prospects by making **pejorative** remarks about each other.

My link:

PERVERSION deliberate unacceptable behaviour (n)

How it is used: That he had committed the murder, was understandable, but that he had disfigured the face so brutally, only indicated some kind of **perversion**.

My link:

PETULANT peevish, bad-tempered (adj)

How it is used: The marooned passengers had full right to behave **petulantly** since they had been sitting at the airport for two days without much help from the airport authorities.

My link:

PROMISCUOUS indiscriminate, casual. (particularly sexually) (adj)

How it is used: Her **promiscuous** lifestyle looked very attractive initially, but soon landed her into a deadly mix of drugs and underworld activities.

My link:

PUGNACIOUS eager to quarrel or argue (adj)

How it is used: The local bully in the village was known to scare all the boys away with his **pugnacious** attitude.

My link:

RANCOROUS bitter, resentful (adj)

How it is used: The divorce proceedings turned **rancorous** as both parties resorted to calling names and abusing each other.

My link:

RECALCITRANT stubborn, obstinate, unco-operative (adj)

How it is used: Even when the union leaders and management reached a settlement, the **recalcitrant** employees refused to join work.

My link:

REPREHENSIBLE deserving censure or condemnation (adj)

How it is used: Killing innocent people and targeting civilians is a **reprehensible** thing to do even in a war.

My link:

REPROBATE an unprincipled person (n)

How it is used: Once he lost heavily in business, he seemed to lose all sanity and decency and turned into quite a **reprobate**.

My link:

SARDONIC mocking or cynical (adj)

How it is used: It was impossible for the new wife to settle down comfortably in her husband's house due to the **sardonic** comments of his mother.

My link:

SCHISM differences in opinion or belief (n)

How it is used: Why should there be so much **schism** between different faiths when ultimately they all lead us to the same God?

My link:

SPECIOUS superficially plausible but actually wrong (adj)

How it is used: The thief kept on arguing, thinking he could convince the police officers not realising they knew that his arguments were totally **specious**.

My link:

TREPIDATION some kind of fear or apprehension (n)

How it is used: People who have experienced some kind of a natural disaster like an earthquake or a tsunami, live in **trepidation** of its recurrence for a long time.

My link:

UMBRAGE sense of offence or annoyance (n)

How it is used: There was no need for Jessica to take **umbrage** to David's remarks as they were meant to check her wayward behaviour.

My link:

UPBRAID scold or reproach (v)

How it is used: The boys found loitering outside the classroom were severely **upbraided** by the headmaster.

My link:

VENDETTA blood fued due to vengeance (n)

How it is used: Many young lives have been lost in the medieval times in several families due to **vendetta**.

My link:

VICARIOUS — acting or done for another (adj)

How it is used: Those who can't sit on dangerous rides in amusement parks, due to whatever reason, find **vicarious** pleasure in seeing others shriek and yell out of excitement and thrill.

My link:

VILIFY — abuse or slander (n)

How it is used: Michael became so desperate to grab the contract that he did not mind even **vilifying** his competitor's reputation.

My link:

VITUPERATIVE — bitter and abusive (adj)

How it is used: What had started as a face off between two high school bullies soon turned out of hand with each getting more **vituperative** and violent.

My link:

WRANGLE — long dispute or argument. (v or n)

How it is used: Once the old duke died, the whole family **wrangled** over the inheritance of his fortunes.

My link:

PRACTICE EXERCISE

Fill in the grid with the correct options in the blank spaces.

WORDS	SYNONYMS	ANTONYMS
1. wrangle	____________	resolve
2. vituperative	abusive	____________
3. vilify	____________	make famous
4. vicarious	____________	by own self
5. vendetta	____________	forgiving
6. upbraid	scold	____________
7. umbrage	annoyance	____________
8. trepidation	____________	fearless
9. specious	____________	true
10. schism	____________	unity
11. sardonic	satiric	____________
12. reprobate	____________	man of principles
13. reprehensible	____________	likeable
14. rancorous	____________	forgiving
15. pugnacious	quarrelsome	____________
16. perversion	unacceptable behaviour	____________
17. pejorative	contemptuous	____________
18. ostracize	exclude from society	____________
19. morbid	abnormal	____________
20. invective	praise	____________
21. insouciant	____________	concerned
22. insolent	____________	polite
23. ingrate	____________	grateful
24. grimace	____________	smile
25. fractious	irritable	____________

WORDS	SYNONYMS	ANTONYMS
26. flagrant	blatant	______________
27. execrate	hate	______________
28. exasperate	______________	alleviate
29. exacerbate	______________	improve
30. disparage	degrade	______________
31. diatribe	______________	praise
32. desultory	purposeless	______________
33. despicable	______________	likeable
34. deplorable	______________	admirable
35. deleterious	______________	beneficial
36. caustic	cutting, biting	______________
37. brusque	blunt, abrupt	______________
38. appalling	______________	pleasing
39. acrimony	______________	friendship
40. acerbic	acidic, sharp	______________

REVIEW EXERCISE–1

Choose the word which fits in best in the given blank in each sentence.

rancorous, pugnacious, schism, exacerbated, fractious, exasperated, ostracism, pejorative, contention, brusqueness, vendetta, despicable, perverted, acrimonious, vicarious, deleterious, execrate, grimace, vituperative, caustic, wrangling, disparaging, morbid, diatribe, insouciant, flagrantly, promiscuous, reprehensible, irascibility, grimace.

1. Their relationship had become quite ______________ with each calling the other names, and alleging unfaithfulness, that they decided to part ways.

2. David could not understand what the ______________ was, if he had decided to leave Chelsea club and play for Manchester United.

3. Since the new boss was not familiar with her nature, her ______________ cost her job.

4. Ever since the once reigning film star started slipping in popularity, he got ______________ satisfaction in seeing other heroes' movies flopping.

5. Carolina's desire for ____________ brought about the destruction of two families.

6. Smith's ____________ language always landed him in trouble, in spite of the best of his hard work in the office.

7. If only humans stopped ____________ ever petty possessions, and could see how beautiful life in itself is.

8. Whenever anything good happened to anybody in their extended family Wren tried to undermine it making ____________ comments and cutting remarks.

9. He was unable to understand why marrying against his parents' wishes could be considered as a ____________ move, as if he had brought bad name to the family or committed a crime.

10. Once the government declared the strike of the mining employees unlawful, the situation which could have improved with negotiations only got ____________.

11. Great thinkers have said, ____________ the crime, not the criminal.

12. Treating the poor people inhumanly and meanly is a ____________ act.

13. The remarks Deborah's boss made in front of the whole staff were always ____________ and insulting.

14. The Board members felt that the CEO should not have indulged in unnecessary ____________ against the functioning of the company in general, and rather concentrated on specific issues and main trouble-makers.

15. Though the government had suppressed the pro-democracy agitation with a heavy hand, the situation was still quite ____________ and peoples' tempers were still simmering.

16. Everyday Samantha delayed and ____________ everybody with her disorganised habits, and procastrinating attitude.

17. She thought she was a super model, and no one could replace her but her ____________ actually gave them a reason enough to fire her and find a new face.

18. When one is in lime-light one has to learn to become ____________ towards criticism, press comments and peering eyes of people.

19. In spite of his tender age he took the painful chemotherapy sessions without a ____________ or a frown.

20. James Peterson had strange, ____________ taste for collecting skulls, bones of animals, their skins and teeth and other such horrific items.

21. In olden times, social ____________ was a popular way of punishing people if they did something which the community disapproved of.

22. When Gabriel's laptop was scrutinised, it was full of pornographic material, a sign of his ____________ mind.

23. One ______________ remark from the editor in his column about the communist party supremo cost him his job.

24. Even though the External Affairs Ministry knew that Pam Pharmaceuticals had ______________ misused the foreign exchange laws, it was powerless to do anything.

25. Once the two brother's families fought over land distribution, their relation always remained ______________.

26. There is a huge divide between the Eastern and Western world, West thinks East is too conservative and backward, East finds Western lifestyle too liberated and ______________.

27. She had a reputation of picking up fights with everyone at her college, and people were tired of her ______________ behaviour.

28. Because of the aunt's ______________ none of the nephews ever went near her or spoke to her.

29. The murder had been done in such a ______________ manner that even the police wondered whose mind could be so psychopathic and perverted.

30. Is it true that ______________ in society between the rich and poor is increasing or is it just a desire to possess more and more.

REVIEW EXERCISE–2

(a) Find words from the main list itself which mean the same as given.

SYNONYMS

1. caustic ______________
2. invective ______________
3. despicable ______________
4. perverted ______________
5. rancorous ______________
6. invidious ______________

(b) Given below are definitions of words or their opposites. Given in the box are the words which have to be written in front of their correct options. Choose the right word.

specious, trepidation, upbraid, wrangle petulant, vilify, contumacious, umbrage, vendetta, vicarious.

1. stubborn or disobedient ______________
2. bad-tempered ______________
3. abuse or slander ______________
4. without fear ______________
5. true, plausible ______________
6. feeling offended ______________
7. violent form of revenge ______________
8. admire, praise ______________
9. done for oneself ______________
10. a fighting or argument ______________

Ch:21

POSITIVITY & PRAISE —Think well, do good, be optimistic

ACCLAMATION enthusiastic public praise (n)

How it is used: The **acclamation** that Satyajit Ray received for his movies made everyone sit up and take notice of his work.

My link:

We did not even know we had a genius amongst us, till the articles Danish wrote on cybertronics began to be **acclaimed** worldwide.

ACCOLADES award in recognition of merit (n)

How it is used: The movie which was a wild-card entry at the International Film Festival surprised everyone by winning the most **accolades**.

My link:

I felt very proud when my town was in news because its athletes had the distinction of winning maximum **accolades** at the olympics.

ACME highest point of achievement (n)

How it is used: The year he won five gold medals in swimming, people thought he had reached the **acme** of his career till he bettered his own record and won seven medals the next year.

My link:

ADULATION excessive admiration (n)

How it is used: Till the pop star was at his peak, he was surrounded with millions of fans who showered him with **adulation**.

My link:

ADVOCACY supporting a cause or policy (n)

How it is used: It is high time more people, social work organisations and corporates began the **advocacy** of environmental causes to stem the degradation.

My link:

AGGRANDIZE artificially enhance the power and reputation of (v)

How it is used: Since it was ruled by the military, in any case, the general **aggrandized** his power to become the ruler of the country.

My link:

ALTRUISTIC selfless, generous (adj)

How it is used: In today's materialistic world it is difficult to determine who is into social work for **altruistic** reasons and who is only looking at publicity and personal mileage.

My link:

AMELIORATE make better, reduce undesirable effect (v)

How it is used: Sam's kind words were successful in **ameliorating** the situation and filling the vacuum she felt after her husband's death.

My link:

APLOMB self-confidence, assurance (n)

How it is used: It was difficult to understand how even in these lean times, the new airline company could talk of profits with such **aplomb**.

My link:

APPEASE placate by acceding to demand (v)

How it is used: The government is constantly walking a tight-rope between bailing out measures for the economy or bowing into **appeasement** under pressure from certain lobbies of industry.

My link:

APPROBATION approval, praise (n)

How it is used: Catherine kept postponing her marriage because it was important for her that she got her father's **approbation** for the partner she had chosen.

My link:

ARMISTICE truce (n)

How it is used: As World Peace Day approached near there was pressure on the two countries to stop aggression and declare **armistice**.

My link:

ASSUAGE make less unpleasant (v)

How it is used: The political leaders swarmed into the hurricane stricken town to **assuage** the misery of the affected people.

My link:

AUGUST inspiring respect and admiration (adj)

How it is used: Even in his nineties, the founder of the company had an **august** personality.

My link:

AUSPICIOUS favourable (adj)

How it is used: The farmers waited for **auspicious** weather conditions to sow their seeds.

My link:

AUTHENTICATE — to prove genuine (v)

How it is used: All suspicions of the Dan Bolt family were put to rest when the will of late Dan Bolt senior was **authenticated** by both his lawyers, and the Bank Manager.

My link:

BLANDISH — coax with kind words, flattery (v)

How it is used: Sara tried to **blandish** her mother into letting her stay the night over at her friend's place but her mum was firm with the curfew hours.

My link:

CLEMENCY — mercy (n)

How it is used: Inspite of the war-like situation it was expected that both sides would show **clemency** to civilian prisoners who had been caught fishing in each other's waters.

My link:

COMMENDATION — formal praise, recommend as good (n)

How it is used: Janel's college principal had given her such a wonderful letter of **commendation** that she knew it would get her a seat at Yale that she so badly wanted.

My link:

COMPLAISANT willing to please others (adj)

How it is used: Duvon was not even aware how people took advantage of her **complaisant** nature and made fun of her behind her back.

My link:

CONCILIATORY placate, pacifying (adj)

How it is used: Suzy was not sure if Dane was making **conciliatory** comments to make up with her or it was another of his smart move to get some more money out of her.

My link:

CONSUMMATE
- showing great skill and flair (adj)
- make relationship complete (v)

How it is used: The pilot steered the aircraft between high buildings on both sides and made emergency landing on the Hudson river with great **consummate** skill and precision.

My link:

CYNOSURE centre of attention or admiration (n)

How it is used: The new supermodel was the **cynosure** of the whole marketing world waiting to grab her for their product endorsements.

My link:

EPITOMÈ — perfect example of a quality or type (n)

How it is used: Several hollywood heroes have portrayed roles which have been **epitomès** of perfect gentlemen for generations to remember.

My link:

ESPOUSE — adopt or support a cause (v)

How it is used: Giving up her successful career of an investment banker on Wall Street, Greta decided to **espouse** the cause of street children in Asian countries.

My link:

EULOGISE — praise highly (v)

How it is used: It was not at all necessary to **eulogise** the new President even before he had even entered the White-House.

My link:

EXEMPLARY — very good, serving as a desirable model (adj)

How it is used: Ramjin, considered to be the meekest boy in the class, showed **exemplary** courage in saving little children from the raging fire in the school.

My link:

EXTOL praise enthusiastically (v)

How it is used: Everyday we hear contradictory reports; one day to **extol** the virtues of new gadgetry, the next day to reveal its harmful effects on people's health.

My link:

IMPECCABLE of highest standards (adj)

How it is used: Andy's work, even as a child was so **impeccable**, notebooks so neat that his classmates wondered how he managed to do it.

My link:

KUDOS praise and honour (n)

How it is used: People who make big in life inspite of handicaps like illiteracy and poverty definitely deserve all **kudos**.

My link:

LAUDATORY expressing praise and commendation (adj)

How it is used: The **laudatory** speech given at the Golden Jubilee celebrations of the military school enthused the cadets to continue the glorious tradition.

My link:

LIONIZE treat as a celebrity (v)

How it is used: It felt strange to Cassius that the same neighbourhood where he was ridiculed had now turned out in large members to **lionize** him for his success in the World Boxing Championship.

My link:

PAEAN a song of praise or triumph (n)

How it is used: The victorious army was welcomed by the kingdom wearing a festive look and people singing **paeans**.

My link:

PALLIATE make less severe, mitigate (v)

How it is used: She could not cure the disease her friend was suffering from, but she could definitely **palliate** her pain, by being with her.

My link:

PANEGYRIC a speech or text in praise of someone/something (n)

How it is used: Once the small check dam was completed by the villagers, the same politicians who had refused to fund it, came in large numbers to indulge in lengthy **panegyrics** appreciating the villagers' efforts.

My link:

PARADIGM — model, a typical example pattern (n)

How it is used: The little solar power station made by indigenous technology of the local talent became a **paradigm** to be copied by many surrounding towns.

My link:

PARAGON — perfect (n)

How it is used: Was she really a **paragon** of all virtues, or put up a near perfect pretense was a mystery in itself.

My link:

PENCHANT — strong liking (n)

How it is used: His **penchant** for mountaineering took him to several countries, scaling one peak after another.

My link:

PLAUDIT — approval, applause (n)

How it is used: Though the director was aware that he had done a good job, yet even he was caught by surprise at the **plaudits** he received from all quarters for the beautiful film.

My link:

PROBITY — honesty and decency (n)

How it is used: The judge promised to uphold the sancity of the chair and investigate into the scandal with all **probity**.

My link:

PUNCTILIOUS — showing great attention to detail or correct behaviour (adj)

How it is used: Bob's parents were worried if his **punctiliousness** would stand in his way of survival in hostel conditions, where four boys would have to co-exist in one room.

My link:

PRACTICE EXERCISE

Fill in the grid with the correct options in the blank spaces.

WORDS	SYNONYMS	ANTONYMS
1. punctilious	___________	careless
2. probity	___________	dishonesty
3. plaudit	___________	disapproval
4. penchant	___________	strong disliking
5. paragon	___________	imperfect
6. paradigm	___________	N/A
7. panegyric	text praising something	___________
8. palliate	___________	increase
9. paean	___________	N/A
10. lionize	treat as important	___________
11. laudatory	___________	defamatory
12. kudos	appreciation	___________
13. impeccable	perfect	___________
14. extol	praise highly	___________
15. exemplary	exclusive	___________
16. eulogy	high praise	___________
17. espouse	___________	not support
18. epitomè	model	___________
19. cynosure	___________	neglected
20. consummate	perfect, complete	___________
21. conciliatory	pacifying	___________
22. complaisant	___________	displeasing
23. commendation	praise	___________
24. clemency	___________	cruelty
25. blandish	___________	dissuade
26. authenticate	___________	prove false

N/A: Not applicable

WORDS	SYNONYMS	ANTONYMS
27. auspicious	___________	unfavourable
28. august	___________	unimpressive
29. assuage	___________	provoke
30. armistice	truce	___________
31. approbation	___________	disapproval
32. appease	placate	___________
33. aplomb	___________	lack of confidence
34. ameliorate	___________	aggravate
35. altruistic	___________	selfish
36. aggrandizement	increase reputation of	___________
37. advocacy	support a cause	___________
38. adulation	admiration	___________
39. acme	peak	___________
40. accolades	___________	brick bats
41. acclamation	public praise	___________

REVIEW EXERCISE–1

Choose the word which fits in best in the given blank in each sentence.

august, cynosure, probity, plaudits, palliative, espousing, armistice, complaisant, exemplary, paeans, impeccable, panegyrics, commendation, conciliation, approbation, extolling, lionized, advocacy, kudos, appease, punctilious, paradigm

1. ___________ the cause of refugees affected by internal strife or terrorism has been the mission of some popular NGOs.
2. The little boy showed ___________ courage while saving his infant sister from the tiger's attack.
3. The new performer at the reality show on TV was the ___________ of all eyes.
4. ___________ of praise followed when the new actor performed the role of the villain in the James Bond movie.
5. The investigation into the multi-billion housing scandal needed to be conducted with complete ___________.
6. The letter of ___________ given by the CEO to a new trainee spoke of his hard work and complete dedication to the job.
7. The UN intervened and put pressure on both countries to stop escalating tension at the border and declare ___________ .
8. The judge was in a ___________ mood and agreed to give bail to the convict in order to meet his new-born daughter.
9. Everyone seemed to be talking about the Booker Prize winning author who was getting ___________ from all critics for his debut novel.
10. The new athlete was chosen to represent the country because he had an ___________ record, not tainted by any drug abuse.
11. The couple had been estranged for several years but agreed to think about ___________ for the sake of their daughter who was suffering from a life-threatening disease.
12. A new drug was launched in the market ___________ its virtue for old people suffering from bone-loss.
13. Lengthy ___________ were printed on leaflets to be distributed amongst the public about the senator's good work before he contested for re-election.
14. Why are film actors, sports person and pop-stars ___________ by every society as if they are super-human.

15. The child prodigy deserved all __________ for his capability to play several musical instruments without any formal training.

16. In order to __________ the crying child the parents decided to buy the expensive toy-car she was demanding.

17. The landlady was absolutely __________ about the tenants coming back before a specified time and locking the main gate behind them at night.

18. The new solar power station became a __________ for more such small-scale ventures in order to make villages self-sufficient in power generation.

19. __________ of human rights protection for war-widows has resulted in women getting education and becoming self-dependent in many S. East Asian nations.

20. Due to the __________ of the new Principal, the college was able to get a completely new wi-fi enabled library.

21. The holy ceremony was graced by the __________ presence of the Pontiff himself.

22. The pain killers could not bring his severed limb back but definitely worked as __________ both to his hurting body and grieving mind.

REVIEW EXERCISE–2

Below are given certain set of words which mean more or less the same. In the box are given certain qualities which are associated with these words. Find the appropriate quality and write in the blank space.

(A) Formal Praise (B) Support (C) Peace (D) Role-Model (E) Please, Pacify (F) Extreme Appreciation (G) Perfect

1. paean, panegyric, extol, eulogy __________
2. paragon, paradigm, exemplary, acme __________
3. epitome, impeccable, consummate __________
4. complaisant, appeasing, conciliatory, assuaging, ameliorating, palliating __________
5. armistice, clemency __________
6. commendation, kudos, laudatory, plaudit, acclamation, adulation __________
7. espouse, advocate __________

Ch:22 SCIENCE & TECHNOLOGY —How geeky are you?

ALCHEMY — a medieval form of chemistry trying to convert base metals into gold or silver (n)

How it is used: Those who practised **alchemy** at that time actually thought it was real and possible.

My link:

If my mother could, she would change all her artificial jewellery into real by using **alchemy**.

AUTOMATON — a mechanism that imitates human actions through coded instructions (n)

How it is used: Even before robots became a reality scientists were toying with the idea of having simplistic **automatons**.

My link:

Though I can't afford a robot, I wish I had alteast an **automaton** which could do some of my work.

EMBRYONIC — at an elementary stage (adj)

How it is used: The research on cloning is now past its **embryonic** stage.

My link:

FERMENTATION — a chemical process used for making wines, beers, alcohol etc., agitation and social unrest (n)

How it is used: The **fermentation** in the neighbourhood after the death of their local leader was palpable, keeping the police on their tenterhooks.

My link:

FULCRUM — the point against which a lever is placed, vital point (n)

How it is used: The debate at the board-meeting veered from the **fulcrum** of the discussion to unnecessary mud slinging.

My link:

FUMIGATE — disinfect or purify with fumes of chemicals (v)

How it is used: After the earthquake the government decided to **fumigate** the town so as to kill any virus and bacteria which may have developed due to so many deaths.

My link:

FUNICULAR — relating to rope or its tension (adj)

How it is used: A special **funicular** train called the Peak Tram goes to Victoria Peak in Hong-Kong.

My link:

FUSELAGE main body of an aircraft (n)

How it is used: The **fuselage** of the crashed aircraft fell miles away from the site of the accident.

My link:

FUSILLADE series of quick gun-shots, volley of questions (n)

How it is used: The press-conference ended with a **fusillade** of questions on the scam from the reporters, which the minister chose not to answer.

My link:

GALVANIZE shock or excite into action, to coat with zinc (v)

How it is used: Before the election, the party leaders **galvanized** the members into action.

My link:

GENEOLOGY study of line of descent (n)

How it is used: The **geneology** of apes and humans is known to have many similarities.

My link:

HALLUCINATION perception of something not present (n)

How it is used: LSD is a **hallucination** inducing drug, and hence dangerous for body's mechanism.

My link:

INCIPIENT at an initial stage; beginning to develop (adj)

How it is used: It was necessary to curb the rebellion in the army while it was still **incipient** and manageable.

My link:

INCUBATE to sit on eggs to keep them warm, to develop slowly e.g. an infectious disease (v)

How it is used: The virus of AIDS **incubates** slowly for a long time, before, the disease becomes apparent.

My link:

KALEIDOSCOPE Constantly changing pattern e.g. of colours (n)

How it is used: The children's costumes at the annual-day function were a **kaleidoscope** of colours.

My link:

KINETIC relating to or resulting from motion (adj)

How it is used: The scooter continued to move even after applying brakes due to its **kinetic** energy.

My link:

LEVITATE rise or cause to rise/hover in the air (v)

How it is used: Certain yogic exercises are so powerful that they can make people light enough to **levitate** in the air.

My link:

MATRIX point of origin/an environment in which something develops (n)

How it is used: The **matrix** of the problem in the hardware system could not be understood by anyone.

My link:

MOMENTUM quantity of motion of a body, force or impetus (n)

How it is used: The workers' strike lost **momentum** once the union leaders joined hands with the management.

My link:

NAUTICAL relating to navigation, maritime (adj)

How it is used: A country's boundaries in the sea extend to several **nautical** miles.

My link:

PROJECTILE something that propels or projects forward e.g. a missile (n)

How it is used: Both launching devices and **projectiles** are increasingly becoming more lethal and accurate.

My link:

PROPELLANT something that pushes or projects forward (n)

How it is used: The **propellants** are being made more and more efficient to give better thrust to the jet engines.

My link:

SPECTRUM band of colours produced when a beam of light is passed through prism; entire range of something (n)

How it is used: The rainbow was so clear and beautiful that the whole **spectrum** of colours was distinctly visible.

My link:

TORQUE — a force that causes rotation (n)

How it is used: He applied **torque** on the wrench to loosen the rusted nut.

My link:

TRAJECTORY — the path of a moving object or a projectile (n)

How it is used: The ball thrown from the building followed a parabolic **trajectory**.

My link:

TRANSLUCENT — semi-transparent (adj)

How it is used: The activities inside the house were dimly visible behind the **translucent** curtains.

My link:

VOLATILE — evaporating rapidly, explosive, unpredictable (adj)

How it is used: The situation all over the world is **volatile**, with complete radicalisation of certain communities and distrust of each other setting in.

My link:

PRACTICE EXERCISE

Match the definitions with the given words.

Column A	Column B
1. torque	(a) something that drives forward
2. trajectory	(b) point of origin
3. translucent	(c) hatch, to develop slowly
4. projectile	(d) float in the air
5. propellant	(e) to coat with zinc
6. nautical	(f) main body of aircraft
7. momentum	(g) to convert base metals into silver
8. levitate	(h) entire range of something
9. matrix	(i) a missile
10. incubate	(j) relating to navigation
11. kaleidosope	(k) a force that causes rotation
12. kinetic	(l) evaporating rapidly
13. hallucination	(m) mechanism that imitates human actions
14. galvanize	(n) beginning to develop
15. geneology	(o) the path of a moving object
16. fusillade	(p) disinfect with fumes of chemicals
17. fuselage	(q) agitation and social unrest
18. embryonic	(r) semi-transparent
19. funicular	(s) firing or outburst
20. fulcrum	(t) perception of something not present
21. fumigate	(u) vital, main point
22. fermentation	(v) quantity of motion of a moving body
23. incipient	(w) relating to rope, operated by cable
24. automaton	(x) producing motion
25. volatile	(y) at an early stage
26. alchemy	(z) study of lineage or descent
27. spectrum	(a^1) changing pattern of colours

REVIEW EXERCISE–1

Choose the word from the box which fits in best in the given blank in each sentence.

geneology, volatile, fumigate, matrix, torque, fermenting, matrix, fulcrum, funicular, propellant, levitating, fuselage, incubate, galvanized, embryonic, projectile, nautical, momentum, hallucination, translucent.

1. On their camping trip, the boys decided to remove the big boulder lying in the middle by using a big rod as a lever and a loose milestone as a ____________ .
2. A lot of engineering marvel was achieved by using ____________ railways to reach low mountain peaks and steep hills.
3. The location of the bomber aircraft was calculated by seeing the ____________ of the missile.
4. The ____________ wings of the dragon-fly shimmered against the morning light.
5. The fire was more devastating because the ____________ fuel stored in he yard caught fire within seconds of the spark.
6. It was an amaging feat that the adolescent swimmer swam the channel which spanned several ____________ miles.
7. It is the finest trick of magincians to show either a member of their troupe or someone from the audience ____________ in the air.
8. The government realised too late that the people's ire aganist constant price rise should have been handled while it was still ____________.
9. In this age of fast production, even the hens are not allowed to ____________ their eggs in a free, natural environment, for sufficient time.
10. When the man woke up, he could not understood if what he had been seeing was a ____________, or a real occurrence. Had he actually seen aliens roaming around the naval base?
11. When steel had not become so popular and so inexpensive, a lot of ____________ iron was used for the same purposes.
12. Wouldn't it be wonderful if ____________ actually became true and base metals could be turned into gold and silver? Nobody would be poor then.
13. The ____________ of the bomber craft was salvaged to determine whether the crash was due to sabotage or an accident.
14. The board of members were asked to look at the whole ____________ of the company's products and their market value before deciding to withdraw a few.
15. The ____________ of the tornado was such that within minutes the whole resort town looked devastated and ravaged.

16. The rat-menace became so unbearable that the mayor decided to ____________ the whole village in order to drive them away.

17. The ____________ of birds has been deeply studied to find the link between their evolution from dinosaurs.

18. It was rumoured that the wrestler was so strong that he could apply ____________ equal to two machines.

19. There was so much of humidity in the tropical rain forest that the vegetation seemed to be ____________ in the hot sun.

20. After the gang-war came out in the open the situation became so ____________ that curfew had to be clamped in the area.

REVIEW EXERCISE–2

Given in front of each word is an option which could either be a synonym or an antonym or none. Choose the right option and put S or A or N for each of the following given choices. First one has been done for you.

1.	kaleidoscopic	drab	A
2.	translucent	semi transparent	
3.	fermentation	burning	
4.	momentum	inertia	
5.	levitate	hover in the air	
6.	incipient	ripe, mature	
7.	incubate	keep frozen	
8.	hallucination	illusion	
9.	galvanize	tarnish	
10.	alchemy	turning into base metal	
11.	fusillade	fused material	
12.	spectrum	entire range	
13.	volatile	calm, composed	
14.	fulcrum	vital point	
15.	embryonic	nascent	

Ch:23 SMALL

—Judge me by my size, do you?

ABRIDGEMENT to shorten (a text or film) without losing sense (n)

How it is used: The **abridgement** of voluminous old classics into more racy, contemporary version worked for the publishing house.

My link:

ATTENUATE reduce the strength, effect or value (v)

How it is used: Consistent rains **attenuated** the intense heat and gave some relief to the desert regions.

My link:

ATTRITION wearing away by friction, or pressure, reduction in numbers (n)

How it is used: Employees were worried if the company was closing down because people were being allowed to leave by following a policy of **attrition**.

My link:

BREVITY — concise and exact use of words (n)

How it is used: **Brevity** in putting one's word across has been important in all ages, whether it is through telegram, telephone, e-mail or text messaging.

My link:

COMPENDIUM — a collection of concise information of a larger work (n)

How it is used: On the occasion of the birth centenary of the celebrated author, a **compendium** of all his work in different fields was brought out.

My link:

CONCISENESS — act of being brief and exact (n)

How it is used: **Conciseness** and cohesiveness are two important qualities of a good essay and write-up.

My link:

DIMINUTIVE — extremely small (adj or n)

How it is used: He looked **diminutive** but within his small frame he possessed tremendous energy and persuading powers.

My link:

DWARFISH small in stature (adj)

How it is used: The 21st century models of cars are becoming increasingly experimental with **dwarfish** and compact looks and alternate fuel consumption technology.

My link:

ENERVATE drain energy, weaken (v)

How it is used: Long spell of fever completely **enervated** her.

My link:

EXIGUOUS very small (adj)

How it is used: Life on earth began with **exiguous**, single-cell creatures inhabiting the seas first.

My link:

FLEDGLING

- a young bird (n)
- an unexperienced person (adj)

How it is used: The group of **fledgling** activists was asked to disperse and disband even before it could start its activities.

My link:

INCONSEQUENTIAL not important or significant (adj)

How it is used: Nobody paid attention to Jack Arthur's inputs in the meeting as they knew what he said was quite **inconsequential** as always.

My link:

INFINITESIMAL extremely small (adj)

How it is used: Nano technology is being tried quite successfully to make chips, circuits which should be **infinitesimal** and very light.

My link:

LILLIPUTIAN trivial or very small (adj or n)

How it is used: In front of the newly constructed tower, the tallest residential complex and the other buildings in the city looked **lilliputian**.

My link:

MEAGRE little, lean, not enough (adj)

How it is used: While some people in developed countries waste so much, at the same time, many people in developing countries subsist on **meagre** incomes.

My link:

MEASLY contemptibly small or few (adj)

How it is used: The whole town was quite horrified to hear that the huge mansion had been auctioned for a **measly** amount.

My link:

MICROCOSM encapsulating something large in miniature form (n)

How it is used: The movie was well appreciated by the Jury because it dared to show as a **microcosm** the moral decadence of modern society.

My link:

MIDGET an extremely small person or thing (n or adj)

How it is used: In front of the tallest man of this world, the normal people looked like **midgets**.

My link:

MINION a follower of a powerful person,
a servile dependent (n)

How it is used: It is strange how power has just passed on from kings to politicians with several **minions** following them wherever they go.

My link:

MINUSCULE extremely tiny (adj)

How it is used: Each person's effort towards saving the environment may look **minuscule**, but is a sure step towards the desired destination of a greener Earth.

My link:

MINUTIAE small precise details (n)

How it is used: For a fine craftsman the attention to **minutiae** is what separates him from the ordinary.

My link:

MODICUM a small quantity of something (n)

How it is used: Though the witness's account sounded far-fetched and sketchy but on closer inspection it was revealed that it had certain **modicum** of truth.

My link:

MYOPIC having short-sighted approach or view, lacking vision (adj)

How it is used: The **myopic** handling of the tension between the two countries led to a war-like situation within no time.

My link:

PALTRY — very small amount, meagre (adj)

How it is used: Labour being cheap in the small industrial town, desperate workers agreed to work for a **paltry** sum.

My link:

PETITE — attractively small and dainty (a woman) (adj)

How it is used: Within her **petite** frame lay great resolve and determination for the cause of the downtrodden.

My link:

PLUMMET — decrease rapidly, steep fall (v)

How it is used: After the undershower the temperature **plummeted** so rapidly that people thought winter had arrived early.

My link:

SUCCINCT — briefly and clearly expressed (adj)

How it is used: The minister's opening speech was listened to with great relish as it was **succinct** and hard-hitting.

My link:

TENUOUS very weak, thin (adj)

How it is used: The person who had accidentally fallen from the 17th floor was miraculously alive, hanging **tenuously** to a branch of a tree.

My link:

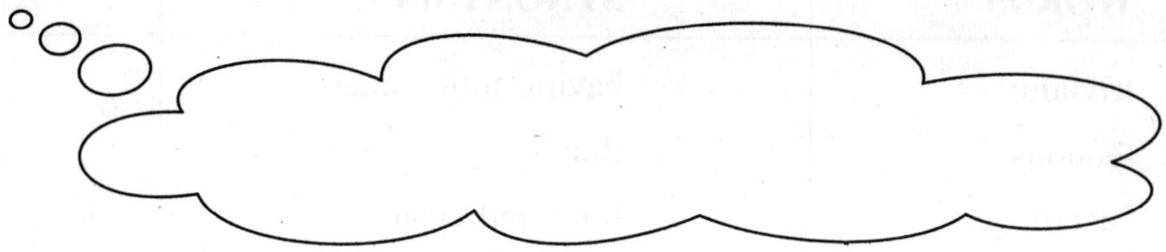

TRIVIALITY of little value or importance (n)

How it is used: Sometimes fretting too much about **trivialities** and unnecessary minute details can delay important projects.

My link:

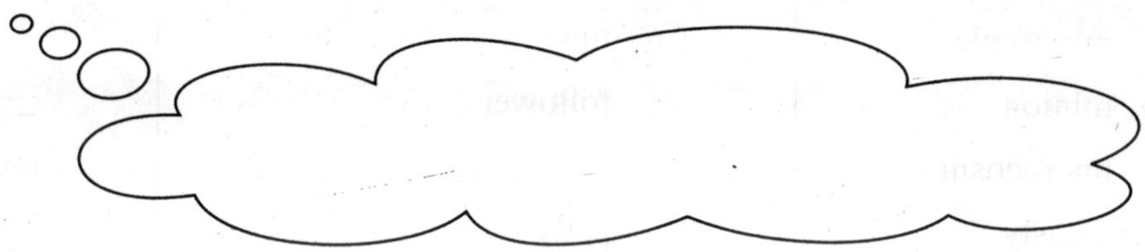

PRACTICE EXERCISE

Fill in the grid with the correct options in the blank spaces.

WORDS	SYNONYMS	ANTONYMS
1. triviality	having little value	______________
2. tenuous	thin	______________
3. succinct	brief and clear	______________
4. plummet	drop	______________
5. petite	small framed, dainty	______________
6. myopic	______________	having foresight
7. modicum	a small quantity	______________
8. minutiae	______________	larger picture
9. minuscule	tiny	______________
10. minion	follower	______________
11. microcosm	______________	macrocosm
12. measly	petty	______________
13. meagre	insufficient	______________
14. liliputian	extremely small	______________
15. infinitesimal	______________	big
16. inconsequential	______________	important
17. exiguous	minute	______________
18. enervate	weaken	______________
19. dwarfish	______________	giant like
20. diminutive	______________	large
21. depletion	______________	accruing
22. constrict	______________	dilate
23. conciseness	in short	______________
24. compendium	______________	N/A
25. brevity	conciseness	______________
26. attrition	______________	increase
27. attenuate	______________	increase
28. abridgement	______________	enlargement

N/A: Not applicable

REVIEW EXERCISE–1

Given along with each sentence are three words. Choose the option which fits in best in the given blanks in the sentences.

1. It was unbelievable that the mugger had killed the elderly man for such a __________ sum of money. (succinct, paltry, dwarfish)
2. Carla and Creg knew they were fighting over something __________ but their egos prevented them from admitting it. (brevily, liliputian, inconsequential)
3. Beauty of something well-written is in its __________ and appropriateness. (compendium, conciseness, abridgement)
4. __________ a text can be a difficult task. One has to retain the essence even in __________. A (abridging, succinct, measly) B (brevity, exiguous, measly)
5. His __________ presence was hardly noticeable till his name was called out on the stage for the year's Achiever's Award. (trivial, diminutive, petite)
6. This year publishers have brought out a __________ of Oscar Wilde's short stories to commemorate his birth centenary. (microcosm, medicum, compendium)
7. The snow began to melt and __________ plants started making appearance as early as January, leading scientists to worry about change in seasonal patterns. (concise, measly, exiguous)
8. The multi national company refused to take up the project because it was __________ for it. (myopic, minuscule, dwarfish)
9. People found it unusual that the tall, dark, handsome hunk of the college should have fallen for the frail, __________ Amanda. (petite, minuscule, paltry)
10. The __________ view of the hard liners has not let development take place in many areas of the Central Asian region. (modicum, minutiae, myopic)
11. If she had even a __________ of decency, she would have said sorry immediately. (modicum, compendium, minuscule)
12. The instructions were quite __________ given to the commoners going for the first space ride to reduce their anxiety and fears. (trivially, succinctly, measly)
13. Many __________ matters about celebrities are reported these days at the cost of real news. (trivial, myopic, microcosmic)
14. What the young writer presented was a __________ of the upwardly mobile section of urban society in many developing countries. (microcosm, minutiae, compendium)

15. Coming from an aristocratic family, she was hardly aware of the __________ of running the household in her marital home. (dwarfish, minutiae, minuscule)

16. The little child was fascinated by the __________ model of a doll-house. (lilliputian, diminutive, microcosm)

17. After the devastating earthquake people were ready to give up their houses for __________ sum of money. (measly, lilliputian, minuscle)

18. People are going for smaller gadgets, and __________ houses to reduce their carbon footprints. (dwarfish, inconsequential, modicum)

19. __________ particles of dust flew as they opened the house which had been closed for several years. (infinitesimal, microcosmic, diminutive)

20. Even before the leader had arrived his __________ were crawling all over the place. (microcosm, minions, midgets)

21. The heat has completely __________ the animals and the poachers are having a field-day being able to trap them easily. (enervated, attenuated, constricted)

22. How could somebody survive on such __________ food and water in the earthquake ravaged house was a miracle. (minuscule, meagre, paltry)

REVIEW EXERCISE–2

Given in front of each word is an option which could either be a synonym or an antonym or none. Choose the right option and put an S or A or N for each of the above given choices. First one has been done for you.

Word	Option	Answer
1. brevity	verbosity	A
2. diminutive	diminishing	
3. exiguous	tiny	
4. inconsequential	insignificant	
5. measly	having smallpox	
6. midget	dwarf	
7. minuscule	minute	
8. myopic	having foresight	
9. succinct	succulent	
10. trivial	petty	
11. petite	broad-built	
12. modicum	decency	
13. microcosm	micro-organism	
14. abridgement	editing	
15. concise	precise	
16. dwarfish	a kind of small fish	
17. lilliputian	imaginary land	
18. paltry	petty	
19. compendium	addition	
20. infinitesimal	infinite	
21. meagre	definite	
22. tenuous	strong	
23. enervate	strengthen	
24. fledgling	chicken	

Ch:24 SORROW —No use crying over spilt milk

AFFLICTION pain, suffering (n)

How it is used: The economists blamed the government's anti-farmer policy for the **affliction** of the people which had led to high prices and scarcity of food grains.

My link: The biggest **affliction** of my country is its increasing population.

AGGRIEVED resentful because of unfair treatment (adj)

How it is used: Everyone present at the funeral of Gordon was surprised to see Eliza, the **aggrieved** ex-wife who had separated from him for several years because of his alcoholism.

My link: My uncle has been **aggrieved** with my father, because he feels he has not got his family rightful share in the property.

BEREAVEMENT deprived of a close one through death (n)

How it is used: His popularity amongst the town folks was evident from the fact that everyone was present to share his grief at this hour of **bereavement**.

My link:

CONTRITION state of feeling remorse (n)

How it is used: In God's eyes feeling **contrition** for one's wrong-doing is enough to seek forgiveness.

My link:

CRESTFALLEN sad and disappointed (adj)

How it is used: As soon as she heard that she had not been selected for the Olympic contingent she was totally **crestfallen**.

My link:

DESOLATE wretched and unhappy (adj)

How it is used: When her young son died in an accident, the mother was **desolate**.

My link:

DESPONDENT loss of hope or courage (adj)

How it is used: She had dreamt all her life of achieving scholarship at the University, yet at the crucial hour of final selection, she appeared listless and **despondent**.

My link:

DISCONSOLATE unhappy, unable to console (adj)

How it is used: Seeing her calf killed by poachers in front of her eyes the elephant cow was **disconsolate**.

My link:

DISPIRITED having lost hope or enthusiasm (v)

How it is used: The contingent at the Olympics put up a very **dispirited** performance, disappointing millions of people back home.

My link:

DOLOROUS feeling great sorrow or distress (adj)

How it is used: The country ballads had an appealing **dolorous** touch to them, and made audience's eyes well up with tears.

My link:

EXCRUCIATE torment physically or mentally (v)

How it is used: When Buddha stepped out of his palace as a young prince, he was **excruciated** to see so much pain and misery due to sickness, old-age and death.

My link:

LAMENT — express regret or disappointment about (v or n)

How it is used: The family feud brought about death and destruction to both the clans and the remaining members had nothing left but to **lament** the loss.

My link:

LANGUISH — grow weak or feeble, be in an unpleasant situation (v)

How it is used: After his wife's death, it was evident that he had lost all desire to live, and seemed to be **languishing**, waiting for his end as well.

My link:

LUGUBRIOUS — mournful, sad, dismal (adj)

How it is used: There was a **lugubrious** air around the abandoned house and gave a creepy feeling to whosoever visited it.

My link:

MAUDLIN — tearfully sentimental (adj)

How it is used: It was strange how a very average and **maudlin** performance by the troupe was so appreciated by the towns folk.

My link:

MELANCHOLY deep sadness (n)

How it is used: Once the news of his being captured by the enemy reached the family of the Air Force pilot, they became riddled with deep **melancholy**.

My link:

MOROSE sullen, grumpy (adj)

How it is used: The London weather was such at the time of his visit, that it made Mr. Grant even more **morose** and sullen.

My link:

PARANOIA unjustified sense of suffering or mistrust (n)

How it is used: It was not clear if the mansion actually had supernatural presence as claimed by Mrs. Bector, or she just suffered from plain **paranoia**.

My link:

PENITENT feeling or showing sorrow and regret, repentant (adj)

How it is used: Though Mr. Brown's son had left the family fold several years ago, they still accepted him when he came back **penitent** and penniless.

My link:

PLAINTIVE sad and mournful (adj)

How it is used: William Wordsworth was very attracted to the Solitary Reaper's **plaintive** song in the poem by the same name.

My link:

REMORSE deep regret or guilt (n)

How it is used: When Sarah realised how she had unnecessarily been in competition with her blind sister, she was filled with **remorse**.

My link:

RUEFUL expressing regret (n)

How it is used: Samantha was **rueful** that she had not tried to stop Roncon when he had walked out on her that night.

My link:

SCOURGE something which causes great trouble (n)

How it is used: Poverty and unemployment are still the **scourge** of many developing countries.

My link:

SOLEMN — dignified and serious (adj)

How it is used: Expecting that the Spire family would start fighting even at the funeral of Mr. Spire, the priest requested them to uphold the sanctity of the **solemn** occasion.

My link:

SOMBRE — dark, oppressive and sober (adj)

How it is used: As the tourists approached the famous medieval castle, they felt a **sombre**, mysterious air about it.

My link:

TRIBULATION — state of great trouble or suffering (n)

How it is used: It is said that it is the trials and **tribulations** of life which make man stronger and wiser.

My link:

WOEFUL — miserable (adj)

How it is used: The **woeful** cries of the villagers struck the air, as they mourned the loss of their near and dear ones due to the terrible cyclone.

My link:

PRACTICE EXERCISE

Choose the word which fits best in the given blank in each sentence.

languished, desolate, aggrieved, sombre, crestfallen, lugubrious, contrite, woefully, dispirited afflictions, bereavement, scourge, disconsolately, lamented, dolorous, rueing, maudlin, morose, plaintive, penitent, tribulations, despondency.

1. Oriental philosophy believes that the more attachments one has, the more ____________ one has, so one is taught to inculcate detachment.
2. The few people that could make it to the island safely after the shipwreck, reached there weary and ____________.
3. As soon as the list of survivors of the air crash was announced, those who couldn't find the names of their loved ones were ____________.
4. By the time he was acquitted of the murder of his neighbour, he had already ____________ in jail for seven years.
5. It was difficult to find why the opposition candidate who had been so aggressive about his victory, suddenly turned so ____________ and dejected.
6. Everyone wondered what Zeba's problem was, to always have a ____________ expression on her face.
7. When the bank declared bankruptcy the ____________ customers staged a sit-out demonstration in front of its headquarters.
8. When Jessie was caught shoplifting, it was evident from her face that she was truly feeling ____________ for the mistake that she had committed.
9. The Swanson's grand wedding had to be postponed because the grandfather passed away and the family was in ____________.
10. The mountain-climbers begin to show signs of ____________ once they began to lose their team-members to frost-bite and bitter cold weather.
11. It was unbelievable how the dog behaved ____________ once its master died in a tragic road-accident.
12. Beatrice ____________ the double loss of both her husband and son at the hands of terrorists.
13. The new opera was a classic ____________ tale of an enmity between two clans leading to the death of the two lovers belonging to the rival families.
14. It was clear that the music wiz was an expert at sentimental songs when he came out with a very ____________ album.

15. After having fought with her boss over a trivial issue Elisa kept feeling ____________ the whole day.

16. The ____________ tone of his piano recital tugged at the hearts of the audience.

17. Julia was not sure if she wanted to accept her husband back when he reappeared after two years looking ____________ and cast down.

18. Alfred Scorcese was known for making movies on dark, ____________ subjects with a twist at the end.

19. The havoc that had been wreaked by the earthquake was ____________ heart-wrenching.

20. Slavery had to be abolished because it had become a ____________ of society.

21. She advised her friend to stop ____________ her break-up which to everyone around looked unevitable from day one.

22. It is important to learn something from the ____________ of life.

REVIEW EXERCISE–1

Now let us see if you are able to recognise the words you have learnt in this chapter. A brief definition and the first letter have been given for your help. First one has been done for you.

1. Somebody who has been wronged is Aggrieved
2. Being lonely and unhappy is D__________
3. Feeling remorse is C__________
4. Having lost hope is being D__________
5. Another word for despair is D__________
6. When you waste away you L__________
7. Lugubrious means the same as D__________
8. If you are showing unjustified fear or sadness you suffer from P__________
9. If you are miserable you must be W__________
10. Another word for very oppressively sober is S__________
11. Dignified seriousness is S__________
12. Pain or suffering can either be affliction or a S__________
13. If you are in a melancholic mood you are feeling P__________
14. If you have lost someone you are B__________
15. If you are in a state of great distress you must be having lot of T__________
16. If you are regretting your actions you must be feeling R__________

REVIEW EXERCISE–2

Given below are words which mean the opposite to the phrases. Fill in the correct option.

scourge, penitent, morose, maudlin, dispirited, crestfallen, disconsolate, desolate, despondent, excruciating.

1. Either you are upbeat or _____________
2. Either you are very motivated or completely _____________
3. Either you are absolutely remorseless or _____________
4. Either you can be easily consoled or you are _____________
5. When you are feeling cheerful you can't be _____________
6. A play can either be slapstick comedy or a _____________ tearjerker.
7. Sometimes we all are happy and comfortable and sometimes just lonely and _____________
8. You can either be very optimistic and hopeful or completely _____________
9. Pain is _____________ while joy is alleviating.
10. Is it true that money is God and poverty a _____________?

Ch:25 VANITY & PRIDE
—No one does better than me

AFFECTATION — something artificially designed to impress (n)

How it is used: People generally avoided going to her lavish parties because of the open air of **affectation** she maintained around her.

My link:

My best friend Jim had an **affectatious** attitude which sometimes led to ego clashes between us.

ARROGANCE — excessive pride in one's own abilities (n)

How it is used: Since Jim came from a small institution where he was looked up by his peers, he developed a certain **arrogance** which did not go well with his classmates at the University.

My link:

My father always taught me that great people showed modesty while empty vessels showed **arrogance**.

AUDACIOUS — rude or disrespectful behaviour (adj)

How it is used: The politician found the reporter's attempt to grill him for the scam in which his name was being dragged, as an **audacious** gesture.

My link:

CHAGRIN annoyance or shame, injured pride (n)

How it is used: As soon as he realised everybody had heard him shout at his family in an inebriated state, he was filled with **chagrin**.

My link:

CHAUVINISM exaggerated patriotism, excessive support for one's own cause (n)

How it is used: Showing **chauvinism** and pretending that they are a superior race does not help the cause of men.

My link:

COMPLACENT uncritically satisfied with oneself, smug (n)

How it is used: In the famous fable the rabbit is shown to be so **complacent** about his victory in the race, that he actually decides to sleep, while the tortoise passes him by in a slow and steady manner.

My link:

CONCEITED excessive pride in oneself (adj)

How it is used: Every body told him he was being **conceited** enough to not realise that the share market was going to crash soon.

My link:

CONDESCENDING showing superiority (adj)

How it is used: His **condescending** attitude even towards his friends alienated him completely.

My link:

CONTEMPTUOUS showing superiority or feeling beneath consideration (adj)

How it is used: When Mike tried to give his boss some suggestions, he just got a **contemptuous** look from the man.

My link:

DESPOTIC very authoritarian and oppressive (adj)

How it is used: The **despotic** king was only hated and feared by his subjects, and nobody cared if he lived or died.

My link:

DISDAINFUL to consider unworthy of one's respect (adj)

How it is used: One of the judges at the beauty pageant was openly **disdainful** of models who were even slightly on the healthier side.

My link:

DOMINEERING	Arrogant and overbearing (adj)
How it is used:	The poor husband had lot of trouble getting along with his **domineering** wife who often nagged him.
My link:	

HAUGHTY	thinking very superior (adj)
How it is used:	The once rich man was too **haughty** to admit that he had fallen on bad days.
My link:	

HUBRIS	Excessive pride or self-confidence (n)
How it is used:	Filled with **hubris**, he ignored his well-wishers' advice, only to fall deeper into the debt-trap.
My link:	

IMPERIOUS	arrogant and dominating (adj)
How it is used:	His **imperious** nature led him to lose the love and affection of everybody near him.
My link:	

IMPERTINENT rude, insolent (adj)

How it is used: Not used to the self-centredness of city-people, the new apprentice at the fashion-house found her colleague's behaviour very **impertinent** and cold.

My link:

INSOLENT rude and disrespectful (adj)

How it is used: Gone are the days when the youngsters could be ticked off for their **insolent** behaviour with older people.

My link:

JINGOISM extreme patriotism (n)

How it is used: If there was any **jingoism** in the Chinese about the grand show they put up at the Beijing Olympics, it could be given to them.

My link:

OFFICIOUS asserting authority (adj)

How it is used: In the absence of the real-incharge of the shop-floor, the assistant took upon himself to show the clients around in a very **officious** manner.

My link:

PATRONIZE — treat kindly with an air of superiority (v)

How it is used: The business tycoon **patronized** the young man with the hope that he would turn into a suitable suitor for his only daughter.

My link:

PEDANTIC — displaying knowledge (adj)

How it is used: A truly scholarly person can never be **pedantic** because he/she doesn't need to.

My link:

POMPOUS — vain and boastful (adj)

How it is used: The starlet who was a wannabe till a day before had suddenly turned into a **pompous** celebrity.

My link:

PRESUMPTUOUS — arrogant (adj)

How it is used: The son accused his parents of having been very **presumptuous** by thinking he was doing well in life, inspite of their never having found time or love for him.

My link:

PRETENTIOUS — trying to pretend superior to what is real (adj)

How it is used: The day the famous Hollywood couple split, each partner cried hoarse about the other's **pretentious** lifestyle.

My link:

SUPERCILIOUS — have an attitude of contempt (adj)

How it is used: Just because he was a struggling painter at a party of renowned artists and painters he was ignored by all in a very **supercilious** manner.

My link:

PRUDISH — excessively modest or proper (adj)

How it is used: It was during the extremely **prudish** Victorian times that British women did nothing but to dress up for tea and dinners in the most elaborate manner.

My link:

SWAGGER — walk or behave arrogantly (v)

How it is used: People at the office knew, the new recruit was related to the boss, as he walked with a definite **swagger**.

My link:

VAINGLORIOUS excessive vanity (adj)

How it is used: Though the film-star was well past his prime, he maintained a **vainglorious** attitude.

My link:

PRACTICE EXERCISE

Fill in the grid with the correct options in the blank spaces.

WORDS	SYNONYMS	ANTONYMS
1. vainglorious	having vanity	____________
2. swagger	walk with arrogance	____________
3. supercilious	contemptuous	____________
4. prudish	having a sense of propriety	____________
5. pretentious	____________	straight forward
6. presumptuous	assuming too much	____________
7. pompous	____________	underestimating oneself
8. pedantic	showing off learning	____________
9. patronize	____________	N/A
10. officious	asserting authority	____________
11. jingoism	extreme patriotism	____________
12. insolent	____________	respectful
13. impertinent	____________	polite
14. imperious	arrogant	____________
15. hubris	self-confidence	____________
16. haughty	arrogant	____________
17. domineering	dominating	____________
18. disdainful	look down upon	____________
19. despotic	____________	democratic
20. contemptuous	beneath respect	____________
21. condescending	showing superiority	____________

N/A: Not applicable

WORDS	SYNONYMS	ANTONYMS
22. conceited	____________	modest
23. complacency	____________	unsure
24. chagrin	annoyance	____________
25. audacious	rude	____________
26. arrogance	____________	modesty
27. affectation	____________	simplicity

REVIEW EXERCISE–1

Choose the word which fits best in the given blank in each sentence.

condescending, domineering, vainglorious, chagrin, audacious, haughtiness, hubris, supercilious, complacency, conceited, contemptuously, jingoism, arrogance, swagger, pompous, impertinent, officious, affectation, patronising, imperious.

1. The father was so ____________ that no one in the family dared open one's mouth to oppose whatever he said.
2. The ____________ attitude of the elite neighbours alienated the poor Joneses further.
3. Much to the professor's ____________ the students decided to walk out of his boring lectures.
4. Snowwhite's step mother was ____________ enough to think she was more beautiful than her step daughter.
5. The father couldn't believe that the son who was a meek gentle creature till yesterday had suddenly turned so ____________ as to bang the door, disregard his concern, and walk out of the house.
6. John had always thought that Sophie loved him too much to ever question his wayward behaviour, but was woken out of his ____________ when she decided to walk out of the marriage.
7. Cinderalla's sisters were jealous of her beauty, but covered it up by behaving extremely ____________ towards her.
8. Betty Sharp's cool ____________ and defiant persona attracted many men towards her.
9. He walked with such a ____________ and ____________ that people wondered who he was and what he was.

10. Everybody agreed that Suzanne was an _____________ fool to have criticized the boss openly at her face.

11. As he became successful in his business ventures he was filled with _____________ at the wealth he had acquired, developing a _____________ attitude towards his old friends.

12. Very few bosses realise that it is not necessary to be _____________ in order to be heard and obeyed.

13. Just because she had been to an elite European finishing school didn't mean she had to acquire an accent, or move around with an air of _____________ .

14. The club's new President who won the elections seemed to be a _____________ man, always talking about the feats he had performed in his earlier capacities.

15. Monica came from a family where there was lot of freedom and democracy, and found Donunique to be a rather _____________ man, choosing to take all major decision on his own.

16. Is it true that celebrities acquire a rather _____________ attitude towards the common people?

17. People could not determine whether it was her _____________ attitude or has aloof nature which was responsible for her silence.

18. When people brag about their country, not ready to see its shortcomings, it is more likely to be considered as _____________.

REVIEW EXERCISE–2

CROSSWORD

Given below is a crossword based on the words just learnt. On the basis of the clues given, fill in the right word.

Across

1. To be authoritarian would be ____________
2. Showing chauvinism about one's country is like showing ____________
3. To be rude is to be ____________
4. Another word for arrogance is ____________
5. Showing too much of pride is showing ____________
6. Some people behave and walk with a lot of ____________
7. Having hubris is being ____________

Down

1. Another word for dominating ____________
2. This person is full of himself ____________
3. Another word for contemptuous ____________
4. Over-confidence in oneself is ____________
5. Being supercilious is to ____________ somebody.
6. To be smug would be to have ____________
7. An impertinent fool would be ____________
8. Somebody who is pretentious is ____________
9. When one's pride is injured one is filled with ____________
10. Being officious is like being ____________.

1. D
2.
3. D
2. J
7. I
5. P
6. C
3. A
4. H
5. A
6.
8. A
7.
9. C
10. I

Ch:26 VIOLENCE —When will man stop fighting?

ANNIHILATION complete destruction (n)

How it is used: Man's systematic **annihilation** of Nature's gifts to mankind is resulting in his own destruction.

My link:

My friend's drug addiction led to complete **annihilation** of his ideals, his achievements, his whole basis of life.

APOCALYPSE destruction, damage on a large scale (n)

How it is used: All the prophecies of an **apocalypse** might actually come true not because of a war but ironically enough, due to environmental disaster.

My link:

After successive earthquakes in my city I feared if we were nearing earth's **apocalypse**.

BLITZKRIEG a swift and intense military action (n)

How it is used: What the government had thought would be a **blitzkrieg** against the rebelling people of the island followed by victory turned into a long drawn exhausting battle.

My link:

BLISTERING intense, vehement (adj)

How it is used: Her **blistering** comments at the new models were not taken too kindly by the fashion agency.

My link:

BLUDGEON a heavy-headed weapon (n or v)

How it is used: The severely mutilated body indicated that the victim had been **bludgeoned** with a club kind of a weapon.

My link:

BOMBARD attack with bombs, constant flow of questions or information (v)

How it is used: At the post-budget press conference, the government officials were **bombarded** with questions related to price increase and inflation.

My link:

BRANDISH to wave something in anger or as a threat (v)

How it is used: The bull **brandished** the horns at the passersby, as if to hit them.

My link:

BRAWL noisy fight or quarrel (n)

How it is used: Several tourists were injured at the drunken **brawl** that broke out in front of the beachside shack.

My link:

BROW-BEAT intimidate (v)

How it is used: Samantha tried to **brow-beat** Susan into helping her at the cafe when she did not want to run it on her own.

My link:

CARNAGE widespread killing (n)

How it is used: Thousands of people lost their lives in the **carnage** that followed at the time of partition of India.

My link:

CATACYLSM violent upheaval or disaster (n)

How it is used: International terrorism is turning out to be quite a **catacylsmic** development of the 21st century.

My link:

CATAPULT a slingshot, a launching device, to move at great speed (n or v)

How it is used: With one victory after another at the races in the Olympic, the athlete got **catapulted** to fame.

My link:

CATASTROPHE disaster, calamity (n)

How it is used: The huge dam, across the river proved to be a **catastrophe** for the area's sensitive seismic placement and triggered a massive earthquake.

My link:

CONFLAGRATION destructive fire (n)

How it is used: Several people died in a **conflagration** which spread into the residential area, spurred by raging fires in the nearby forest-area.

My link:

DETONATION explosion (n)

How it is used: The **detonation** of the atom bomb over Hiroshima and Nagasaki was done several metres above the ground so as to cause maximum destruction.

My link:

DISARMAMENT reduction or withdrawal of military forces (n)

How it is used: Nuclear **disarmament** has at least been able to stop the nuclear arms race to some extent.

My link:

FOMENT instigate or stir up (v)

How it is used: The rebel leader was charged for **fomenting** trouble amongst the tribals against the new government.

My link:

FRACAS noisy quarrel (n)

How it is used: The **fracas** that ensued over a minor property dispute resulted in unnecessary death of two people.

My link:

FULMINATE express vehement protest, explode violently (v)

How it is used: What was simmering as a mild discontent **fulminated** in widespread riots due to the government's callousness.

My link:

HOLOCAUST destruction or slaughter on a large scale (n)

How it is used: The nuclear **holocaust** of the 2nd World War will remain the most dark chapter of World History.

My link:

IMBROGLIO an extremely confused or complicated situation (n)

How it is used: The helpless diplomat was caught in an **imbroglio** initiated by the two countries' military top-brass.

My link:

INCARCERATE imprison or confine (v)

How it is used: The government had no option but to **incarcerate** the protesting workers which angered the striking labour union further.

My link:

INCENDIARY tending to cause conflict, a device to cause fire e.g. a bomb (adj)

How it is used: The arsonists had come with the intention of maximum damage, and had brought **incendiary** material with them.

My link:

LAMBAST criticise harshly (v)

How it is used: The police officer was **lambasted** for misplacing an important document which contained classified information on several criminals.

My link:

MAELSTROM confused upheaval, powerful whirlpool (n)

How it is used: It was not clear why the sleepy little town had been plunged into a **maelstrom** of political intrigue and controversy.

My link:

MUTINOUS rebellions (adj)

How it is used: The soldiers began to turn **mutinous** when they realised they were not being provided any relief against the bitter cold and starvation.

My link:

ONSLAUGHT fierce, dreadful attack (n)

How it is used: The small local army could not withstand the **onslaught** of the king's massive force.

My link:

PAROXYSM — sudden attack or violent expression of something (n)

How it is used: As soon as the news of their leader's death reached the crowd, the people were engulfed with a **paroxysm** of rage and started pelting stones at the doctor's clinic.

My link:

PILLAGE — rob or steal with violence (v)

How it is used: It was difficult to identify the culprits because the whole village had participated in the act of **pillaging** and plundering the neighbourhood market.

My link:

PULVERIZE — reduce to fine particles, defeat utterly (v)

How it is used: The guerilla warfare adopted by the rebels succeeded in **pulverizing** the economy of the country.

My link:

RAMPAGE — rush around violently (v)

How it is used: The biker gang would often go on a **rampage** in the affluent neighbourhood and loot the shops at will.

My link:

SKIRMISH small and irregular fights (n)

How it is used: The people at the border had become so used to regular **skirmishes** that gun-fire hardly evoked any response or surprise.

My link:

TRUCULENT quick to fight (adj)

How it is used: She had a **truculent** nature, because of which her neighbours avoided her.

My link:

TURBULENCE disorder, confusion (n)

How it is used: The internal political **turbulence** of the country had a ripple effect on the international political scene.

My link:

PRACTICE EXERCISE

Now let us see if you are able to recognise the words you have learnt in this chapter. A brief definition and the first letter have been given for your help. First one has been done for you.

1. minor fight — Skirmish
2. rush about violently — R________
3. criticise harshly — L________
4. destruction — A________
5. hit with a blunt, heavy object — B________
6. wave around — B________
7. plunder and loot — P________
8. noisy quarrel, brawl — F________
9. explode thunderousely — F________
10. destruction by fire — H________
11. violent upheaval — C________
12. swift military operation — B________
13. disaster on a large scale — A________
14. explosion — D________
15. extensive fire — C________
16. widespread killing — C________
17. dreadful attack — O________
18. noisy quarrel — B________
19. a sling shot — C________
20. state of unrest, disturbance — T________
21. a confusing complication — I________
22. violent expression of something — P________
23. to incite, instigate — F________
24. reduction or withdrawal of military force — D________
25. calamity — C________
26. rebellious — M________
27. imprison — I________
28. fiery — I________

REVIEW EXERCISE–1

Given along with each sentence are three words. Choose the option which fits in best in the given blanks in the sentence.

1. Fortunately the bomb did not explode because the timer meant to ___________ it did not work. (detonate, disarm, foment)
2. What had started like a local bush-fire soon turned into a major ___________ engulfing the whole area adjoining the forest. (catastrophe, onslaught, conflagration)
3. In the absence of effective policing the local goons began to waylay and ___________ the travellers. (pillage, pulverize, rampage)
4. The river changed its course, breaching the embankments, and rushed into the low-lying areas in a ___________. (paroxysm, maelstrom, onslaught)
5. These days when the stock-market crashes in one country, the ___________ caused in the market because of it is felt even continents away. (turbulence, rampage, catastrophe)
6. After the second world war nuclear ___________ should have become a reality and not just a subject of discussion. (disarmament, holocaust, catapult)
7. The religious leaders were advised to hold dialogue with the hardliners who were ___________ trouble amongst the general public. (pillaging, fomenting, pulverizing)
8. The local tribes were used to minor ___________ which they had settled on their own over the years. (imbroglios, skirmishes, pillage)
9. The ___________ between the two warring gangs seemed to blow up into a gang war. (fracas, catapult, brawl)
10. The monkeys went on a ___________ in the temple-town having been encouraged by the swarm of devotees offering them food. (imbroglio, rampage, pillage)
11. The child was shooting pebbles at the rabbits with a ___________. (catapult, cataclysm, catastrophe)
12. The London fire of 1661 was a ___________ recorded in the history of the city. (holocaust, paroxysm, blitzkrieg)
13. Jack killed his wife Amanda in a ___________ of rage, only to repent lates. (apocalypse, paroxysm, blistering)
14. The bull ___________ its horns so threateningly that the bystanders at the show got scared. (brandished, blistered, bludgeoned)
15. The ravines of the rocky landscape were ___________ in order to flush the terrorists from their hide-outs. (bombarded, annihilated, catapulted)

16. The __________ heat of the summer sun was enough to dry up the throats of the tourists in the tropical country. (blistering, brandishing, catapulting)

17. Roger was a TV presenter, known for his __________ tone in most of the interviews that he held on his show. (truculent, turbulent, foment)

18. More and more people are beginning to believe that __________ of earth is imminent because of man's inability to check carbon emmissions. (annihilation, carnage, catastrophe)

19. The adventurous __________ against the neighbouring country proved very expensive to the belligerent army as it lost many lives. (blitzkrieg, incendiary, pillage)

20. The __________ forces kept increasing in number supported by the native people and rulers. (incendiary,. mutinous, blistering)

REVIEW EXERCISE–2

Given in front of each word is an option which could either be a synonym antonym or none. Choose the right option and S or A or N for each of the following given choices.

1. apocalypse	preservation	☐
2. conflagration	destructive fire	☐
3. foment	ferment	☐
4. holocaust	annihilation	☐
5. onslaught	attack	☐
6. maelstrom	calm	☐
7. pillage	plunder	☐
8. rampage	attack	☐
9. truculent	to avoid fight	☐
10. brow-beat	intimidate	☐
11. turbulence	orderly	☐
12. skirmish	brawl	☐
13. pulverize	grind to particles	☐
14. fulminate	culminate	☐
15. fracas	quarrel	☐
16. detonation	explosion	☐
17. mutinous	supporting	☐
18. incendiary	hydrating	☐

MISCELLANEOUS
—Words that should be remembered

A

abate
aberration
abeyance
abhorrence
abscond
abstemious
acculturate
admonish
adroit
aerate
affirmation
agenda
aggregate
agitate
ambivalent
amble
amenable
analysis
anarchy
anomalous
antagonism
antipathy
apathy
apogee
apposite
apprise
approbate
appropriate (v)
artless
aspersion
audacious
austere
autonomous
aver

B

balmy
banal
barb
behemoth
bellicose
belligerent
beneficient
benevolent
benign
bestial
bizarre
blasphemy
blatant
bleak
bolster
bonanza
boorish
brackish
braggadocio
brazen
burnish
buxom

C

cache
cajole
callous
calumny
candid
cantankerous
carnivorous
carping
castigate
caustic
celibate
centaur
centrifugal
cessation
chameleon
charlatan
chimera
circuitous
circumspect
circumvent
cleavage
cloying
coagulate
comity
commensurate
commiserate
concur
condone
conflate
confound
contend
converge
corroborate
coterie
countenance
covert
crave
credo
crescent
crusade
culpable
cursory

D

decorum
default
default
defer
deference
deft
degraded
delineate
derision
dessicate
deterrent
devoid
dichotomy
diffidence
diffuse
digression
dilate
dimension
disarm
discerning
discordant
discrepancy
discrete
disinterested
disjointed
dismiss
disparate
dispassionate
disquiet
dissemble
diverge
doctrine
dupe
duplicity
duress

E

eccentric
eclipse
efface
effeminate
effete
effigy
egoist
egress
elated
elusive
emanate
embargo
emolument

empirical
enclave
energize
engage
engender
enmity
ennui
equity
eradicate
ethnic
exhume
exigent
expedite
extradite
extrovert

F

facet
facile
facilitate
fallible
falter
fatuous
fawning
feasible
feign
felony
felter
ferment
ferrous
fester
fetish
fiasco
figurative
filch
finale
finite
flaccid
flippant
flout
foible
foray
forestall
forte
foster
frustrate
furtive
futile

G

gainsay
gamut
garbled
gauche
gaudy
generic
genteel
genuflect
germane
germinate
gestation
gesticulate
gnarled
goad
gouge
graphic
grimace
grisly
gruesome
guileless
guise
gullible
gusto
gusty

H

hackneyed
hallmark
haphazard
harass
harbinger
harbour (v)
haven
hazy
hedonist
heinous
heinous
herbivorous
heresy
heterogenous
heyday
hiatus
hirsute
histrionic
homogenous
hone
hostility
hubris
humane
humid
humility
husbandry
hybrid
hypochondriac
hypocritical

I

icon
ideology
idiosyncracy
igneous
ignite
imbibe
imbue
imminent
immune
impair
impartial
impeach
implicit
inadvertent
incorporate
incubation
indictment
indignation
inept
inert
inherent
inhibit
innocuous
innuendo
insinuate
insipid
instigate
intrinsic
inundate
invoke
iota
iridescent
itinerary

J

jaded
jaunt
jettison
jibe
jostle
judicious
juncture
jurisprudence
justification
juxtapose

K

kernel
killjoy
kindle
kindred
kleptomaniac
knead
knoll
knotty

L

labile
labyrinth
laceration
lachrymose
lackadaisical
lackluster
laggard
lassitude
lateral
legacy
lethargic
libido
lineage
lithe
loath
loathe
log
longevity
loom
lumber
luminous
lunar
lunge
lurid
luscious
lustrous
luxuriant

M

magnate
maim
malaise
malign
malignant
malingerer
malleable
mandate
mandatory
mania
manifest
manifesto
mauve
meander
melee
mercurial
mesmerize
metamorphosis
meticulous
milieu
miscreant
modicum
mollify
monolith
moribund
motley
mundane
murky
myriad
mystic

N

naìve
narcissistic
nascent
natal
nautical
necromancy
nefarious
negate
negligible
negotiate
nemesis
neophyte
nexus
nomad
nonchalant
nondescript
nonplus
nostalgia
notable
notoriety
novice
noxious
nuance
nubile
nucleate
nugatory
nullify
nuptial
nurture
nutrient

O

obeisance
obelisk
obese
obituary
objective
obligatory
obnoxious
obsequy
obsessive
obviate
occidental
occlude
odium
officious
olfactory
ominous
omnivorous
onerous
onslaught
onus
opiate
opportune
opprobrium
optimum
opus
orgy
oscillate
ossify
ostracize
outspoken
overt
ovoid
oxidation

P

palatable
paranoia
partisan
pathological
paucity
pedantic
phlegmatic
piety
placate
plagiarize
plasticity
platitude
polemic
porous
portentous
pragmatic
preamble
precarious
precept
precipitate (adj)
precocious
precursor
predilection
presage
presumptuous
proficient
prohibitive
promulgate
propagate
propriety
proscribe
psyche
puerile
purview

Q

quack
quadruped
quaint
quarantine
quarry
quash
queasy
quell
query
quibble
quietude
quirky
quiescent
quiver
quixotic
quotidian

R

rabid
rampart
rapacious
rapprochment
rarefied
rational
recalcitrant
recrimination
recumbent
refractory
refurbish
refute
regimen
relegate
relinquish
remonstrate
rendezvous
reproach
reprobate
repudiate
rescind
resilient
resolution
respite
restive
reticent
reverent
riveting
rostrum
rotunda
rudimentary
rusticate

S

salient
sanction
satiate
saturate

saunter
sceptic
seine
septic
sever
shirk
solicitude
soporific
spectrum
spontaneity
sporadic
stasis
stereotype
stigma
stint
stipulate
stolid
street
striation
subdued
subjective
subside
substantiate
superfluity
supersede
supposition
suppress
sustenance
sweltering
swerve
sybil
synchronise

T

tacit
talisman
tangential
tangible
tantalize
taper
taut
tawdry
tedium
temper (v)
tenable
tender
tenet
tentative
tenure
thermal
thrive
throng
tipple
tome
torpid
torpor
tortuous
transgress
transpire
travesty
tremulous
trilogy
trite

U

ultimatum
umbrage
unanimity
unctuous
underscore
undulation
unearth
unilateral
unique
unison
unkempt
unruly
unseemly
untenable
upbraid
usurp
utopia

V

vacillate
vagary
valedictory
valid
vapid
vehement
venal
vendor
venial
vent
venue
verbiage
verity
vernal
viable
vigilance
vindicate
vindictive
virulent
viscous
vitriolic
vivisection
volatile
volition
voluble
vouchsafe
voyeur
vulnerable
vulpine

W

waif
wane
wanton
warranty
wary
wax (v)
waylay
welter
wheedle
whet
whinny
windfall
withdrawn
withhold
withstand
wizardry
worldly
wrangle
wreak
wrench
writ

Y

yeoman

Z

zenith

SOLUTIONS

CHAPTER 1

Practice Exercise (Page 8)

1. above harm
3. wanderer
4. safe
5. reckless
6. uncertain
7. conformist
8. to put in danger
9. bold
10. random
11. uncertain
12. unplanned
13. thoughtful
14. planned
15. safe
17. by chance
18. to take risk
19. avoid meeting
20. modesty
21. possibility
22. concerned
23. moody
24. immature
25. intentional

Review Exercise–1 (Page 9)

2. D
3. D
4. B
5. B
6. B
7. A
8. C
9. B
10. C
11. E
12. C
13. E
14. E
15. B

Review Exercise–2 (Page 11)

CROSSWORD

ACROSS	DOWN
1. vagabond	1. voyage
2. gambol	2. temerity
3. enterprise	3. capricious
4. encounter	
5. imprudent	

CHAPTER 2

Practice Exercise (Page 21)

1. (e^{1})
2. (z)
3. (d)
4. (w)
5. (r)
6. (f^{1})
7. (j)
8. (y)
9. (m)
10. (g)
11. (c)
12. (b)
13. (f)
14. (d^{1})
15. (t)
16. (p)
17. (x)
18. (o)
19. (q)
20. (k)
21. (s)
22. (h)
23. (e)
24. (i)
25. (u)
26. (a^{1})
27. (v)
28. (c^{1})
29. (b^{1})
30. (a)
31. (l)
32. (n)

Review Exercise–1 (Page 23)

2. C
3. D
4. D
5. B
6. C
7. E
8. B
9. A
10. B
11. E
12. A
13. D
14. D
15. A
16. C
17. A
18. B

Review Exercise–2 (Page 25)

2. mural
3. pantomime
4. raconteur
5. pot-pourri
6. staccato
7. repertoire
8. thespian
9. tutelage
10. visage
11. vignette
12. unison
13. prologue
14. percussion
15. artefacts
16. warble
17. mimicry
18. crescendo
19. mosaic

CHAPTER 3

Practice Exercise (Page 32)

1. embellishments
2. comely
3. diaphanous
4. filligree
5. flawless
6. aesthetic
7. pulchritude
8. florid
9. veneer
10. idyllic
11. winsome
12. pristine
13. picturesque
14. scintillating
15. gossamer
16. ornate
17. immaculate
18. urbane

Review Exercise–1 (Page 33)

CROSSWORD

ACROSS

1. picturesque
2. winsome
3. idyllic
4. flawless
5. aesthetic
6. ornate
7. gossamer

DOWN

1. diaphanous
2. comely
3. embellish
4. filligree

Review Exercise–2 (Page 34)

2. embellish
3. filigree
4. comely
5. immaculate
6. scintillating
7. gossamer
8. pristine
9. florid
10. idyllic
11. veneer
12. winsome
13. picturesque
14. aesthetic
15. flawless
16. pulchritude
17. diaphanous
18. urbane
19. ethereal
20. panache

CHAPTER 4

Practice Exercise (Page 46)

1. polite
2. local language
3. wordy
4. new formation
5. welcome note
6. criticism
7. quiet
8. overt
9. monologue
10. meaningful talk
11. talkative
12. not repeat
13. renounce
14. pithiness
15. formal language
16. art of speech
17. clear
18. talkative
19. speaking a lot
20. simple language
21. praising
22. meaningless talk
23. quiet
24. confuse
25. enlist
26. improvise
27. praise
28. clear expression
29. hide
30. topic related
31. discussion
32. unprincipled talk
33. praise
34. illogical talk
35. informal talk
36. literary
37. connected
38. not making sense
39. weak
40. fluent
41. sour

Review Exercise–1 (Page 48)

2. E	8. A	14. A	20. A	26. C	32. B
3. D	9. D	15. A	21. C	27. A	33. D
4. E	10. B	16. D	22. B	28. E	34. A
5. A	11. A	17. C	23. A	29. C	35. D
6. A	12. A	18. A	24. C	30. B	
7. A	13. A	19. B	25. A	31. A	

Review Exercise–2 (Page 52)

List A

1. taciturn
2. encomium
3. incoherent
4. reticent
5. lucid
6. laconic
7. reiterate
8. tacit

List B

1. acerbic
2. colloquial
3. jargon
4. eloquent
5. reticent
6. prolixity
7. rhetoric

CHAPTER 5

Practice Exercise (Page 64)

1. simple methods
2. fake
3. simple statements
4. praise
5. real form
6. true picture
7. confess
8. speak truth
9. disloyal
10. cheating
11. theft
12. convince
13. speak straight
14. dishonesty
15. true identity
16. illegal
17. honesty
18. show true self
19. false idea
20. artificial
21. true interior
22. cheat
23. revealing truth
24. straight forward
25. tell lies
26. simple, straight forward
27. illusion
28. disbelieving
29. legal bringing of goods
30. co-operate
31. remain apart
32. round about
33. truth
34. true inner self
35. re-affirm
36. cheat
37. truth
38. pretension
39. impure
40. disavow

Review Exercise–1 (Page 66)

1. semblance
2. fraudulent
3. spurious
4. delusion
5. fallacy
6. dubious
7. perjury
8. insinuated
9. larceny
10. stratagem
11. illicit
12. imposter
13. credulity
14. feigned
15. improbity
16. devious
17. simulation
18. contraband
19. adulteration
20. charade

Review Exercise–2 (a) (Page 68)

1. (l)
2. (a)
3. (i)
4. (f)
5. (k)
6. (g)
7. (j)
8. (e)
9. (h)
10. (d)
11. (c)
12. (b)

Review Exercise–2 (b) (Page 69)

1. dubious
2. delusion
3. prevaricate
4. sophistry
5. perfidious
6. perjury
7. inveigle
8. mendacity
9. fallacious
10. adulterate

CHAPTER 6

Practice Exercise (Page 78)

1. energetic
2. dull
3. lifeless
4. manly
5. forceful
6. weak
7. purposeless
8. bravery
9. power
10. cannot be removed
11. feeble
12. tireless
13. strong
14. without force
15. weak
16. dullness
17. calm
18. courage
19. lack of purpose
20. sporadic
21. timid
22. hard working
23. listless

Review Exercise–1 (Page 79)

1. ardour
2. diligence
3. inextricably
4. impetus
5. assiduous
6. trenchant
7. impermeable
8. fortitude
9. impregnable
10. frenzy
11. vitality
12. vehement
13. zealously
14. vivacious
15. potent

Review Exercise–2 (Page 80)

A. a) F b) D c) A d) B e) E f) C

B. CROSSWORD (Page 81)

ACROSS	DOWN
1. potency	1. trenchant
2. zealous	2. ardour
3. diligent	3. virile
4. fortitude	4. frenzy
5. frenetic	5. tenacity
6. vivacious	6. prowess
7. vitality	

CHAPTER 7

Practice Exercise (Page 95)

1. simple
2. deadlock
3. easily understood
4. loner
5. difficulty
6. simple solution
7. no accountability
8. light, easy
9. avoid
10. remain away
11. open
12. remembering something
13. make clear
14. flexible
15. disturbed
16. pose as something
17. hidden
18. complicated
19. willing to change
20. easily solvable
21. pliable
22. tough
23. clear the path
24. deadlock
25. not easily understood
26. entanglement
27. powerful
28. not caring about details
29. above ordinary
30. hide
31. simple and clear
32. burden
33. harsh
34. come to a dead end
35. secretive
36. point of importance
37. simple
38. straight forward
39. open
40. secretive
41. hide
42. hard-working
43. complicated
44. stubborn
45. light-hearted

Review Exercise–1 (Page 97)

1. cryptic
2. impediment
3. crux
4. impervious
5. formidable
6. ensconced
7. reclusive
8. obfuscated
9. imbroglio
10. unobtrusive
11. obviated
12. onerous
13. obdurate
14. predicament
15. esoteric
16. arcane
17. latent
18. uncanny
19. adamant
20. impalpable
21. fastidious
22. draconian
23. clandestine
24. concealed
25. inscrutable

Review Exercise–2 (Page 99)

2. A
3. S
4. S
5. A
6. N
7. N
8. S
9. S
10. A
11. A
12. S
13. A
14. N
15. S
16. A
17. S
18. A
19. A
20. N

CHAPTER 8

Practice Exercise (Page 111)

1. stormy winds
2. peak, top most
3. related to spring
4. wavy
5. swollen
6. murky
7. calm, cool
8. loose
9. earthly
10. balmy
11. flabby
12. not look for
13. destroy
14. strongly smelling
15. result, branch
16. simple
17. rotting
18. reduce
19. steep
20. colourful
21. annual
22. vast expanse
23. related to night
24. zenith
25. reality
26. pleasant
27. quick
28. winding
29. confusion
30. look for
31. dry

Review Exercise–1 (Page 113)

1. precipitous
2. vernal
3. strata
4. pachyderms
5. maelstrom
6. panoramic
7. putrid
8. tempestuous
9. redolent
10. pie-bald
11. tethered
12. sinewy
13. seismic
14. forage
15. arid
16. mirage
17. miasma
18. nocturnal
19. meteoric
20. ephemeral

Review Exercise–2 (Page 115)

1. (h)
2. (p)
3. (l)
4. (q)
5. (g)
6. (c)
7. (m)
8. (n)
9. (j)
10. (o)
11. (b)
12. (f)
13. (r)
14. (d)
15. (e)
16. (a)
17. (k)
18. (i)

CHAPTER 9

Practice Exercise (Page 124)

2. insidious
3. quisling
4. maniacal
5. vindictive
6. diabolic
7. fiendish
8. truculent
9. instigate
10. avarice
11. unscrupulous
12. piqued
13. hedonist
14. turpitude
15. castigate
16. misanthrope
17. miscreant
18. vitiate
19. virulent
20. nefarious

Review Exercise–1 (Page 125)

1. malefic
2. calumny
3. malevolent
4. pernicious
5. instigate
6. truculent
7. unscrupulous
8. hedonist
9. castigate
10. avarice
11. callous
12. pique
13. insidious
14. tirade
15. misanthrope

Review Exercise–2 (Page 126)

1. malefic
2. machiavelean
3. malevolence
4. calumny
5. maniacally
6. pernicious
7. renegade
8. virulent
9. vindictive
10. nefarious
11. sadist
12. fiend
13. callously
14. quisling
15. hedonistic
16. turpitude
17. castigated
18. insidious
19. heinous
20. diabolic
21. instigated
22. avarice
23. truculent
24. piqued
25. unscrupulous

CHAPTER 10

Practice Exercise (Page 134)

1. extreme hunger
2. lukewarm
3. delicious
4. dissatisfy
5. hungry
6. strong smelling
7. worth drinking
8. mildly flavoured
9. swallow fast
10. make better
11. without appetite
12. keep it plain
13. tasteless
14. turn white

Review Exercise–1 (Page 135)

1. pungent
2. leavened
3. mastication
4. condiments
5. glutton
6. voraciously
7. garnishing
8. scrumptious
9. delectable
10. piquancy
11. cuisine
12. gourmand
13. ambrosia
14. manna
15. victuals
16. tepid
17. potable
18. ravenous
19. blanched
20. epicurean's

Review Exercise–2 (Page 136)

2. A
3. S
4. S
5. S
6. N
7. A
8. S
9. S
10. A
11. N
12. N
13. S
14. S
15. A
16. S
17. N
18. S
19. A
20. N
21. S
22. N

CHAPTER 11

Practice Exercise (Page 146)

1. liberal
2. defile
3. localised
4. temporary
5. heavenly
6. sure, confident
7. not sacred
8. disrespectful
9. intrinsic
10. to liberate
11. freedom of religion
12. pure
13. normal
14. unprophetic
15. all knowing
16. normal
17. recital
18. non-believer
19. earthly
20. desecrate
21. collect
22. heavenly
23. boon
24. sceptic

Review Exercise–1 (Page 147)

1. transience
2. ubiquitous
3. litany
4. purgatory
5. sanctimonious
6. preternatural
7. occult
8. venerated
9. temporal
10. benediction
11. zealotry
12. corporeal
13. quintessence
14. profanities
15. tenet
16. sceptical
17. iconoclastic
18. portent

Review Exercise–2 (Page 149)

2. corporeal
3. temporal
4. canon
5. sanctimonious
6. anoint
7. transient
8. proselytize
9. quintessential
10. consecrate
11. oracular
12. congregation
13. omnipresent
14. purgation
15. reverent
16. agnostic
17. benediction
18. ubiquitous
19. apocalyptic
20. portend

CHAPTER 12

Practice Exercise (Page 158)

1. full
2. plenty
3. unfavourable
4. multiply
5. abundance
6. small
7. surfeit
8. more than enough
9. complete
10. simple
11. grandeur
12. many
13. of single kind
14. generosity
15. important
16. small town
17. thinking small
18. huge
19. stinginess
20. unimpressive
21. respected
22. abundant
23. small
24. tiny
25. increasing
26. littleness

Review Exercise–1 (Page 159)

1. mammoth
2. proliferating
3. myriad
4. munificence
5. prodigious
6. opulence
7. profusion

Review Exercise–2 (Page 160)

2. A
3. N
4. N
5. S
6. S
7. S
8. N
9. S
10. S
11. A
12. N
13. S
14. N
15. N

CHAPTER 13

Practice Exercise (Page 171)

1. weep
2. prove unlucky
3. enthusiastic expression
4. mourning
5. sorrowful
6. sorrow
7. sad
8. not funny
9. lack of respect
10. defeated
11. jolly
12. joking
13. unhappy
14. satisfaction
15. cheerful
16. not interested
17. happiness
18. dispirited
19. inappropriate humour
20. lifeless
21. sense of loss
22. exciting
23. extreme sadness
24. displease
25. heavenly
26. sadness
27. bubbly
28. happiness
29. lack of excitement
30. humourless
31. lack of taste
32. cry loudly
33. floating
34. carefree
35. lack of cheer
36. readiness

Review Exercise–1 (Page 173)

1. enthralled
2. revelry
3. alacrity
4. ebullient
5. delectation
6. smirked
7. chortled
8. blithe
9. serendipity
10. buoyant
11. beatitude
12. exhilirating
13. hilarious
14. elation
15. levity

Review Exercise–2 (Page 174)

1. A
2. B
3. E
4. H
5. C
6. D
7. F
8. G

CHAPTER 14

Practice Exercise (Page 175)

1. making ill
2. beneficial
3. pleasant
4. left to die
5. ail
6. keep separate
7. related to mind and body
8. physical ailment
9. depression
10. curative
11. not afraid
12. hyperactive
13. poison
14. pain inducing
15. drug
16. please
17. short-sighted
18. comfort
19. weakness
20. calm, healthy
21. epidemic
22. disturbing
23. not spreading to others
24. full of vigour
25. obsession to lose weight

Review Exercise–1 (Page 184)

1. myopic
2. salutary
3. emollient
4. endemic
5. anorexic
6. infirmity
7. therapeutic
8. phobia
9. epileptic
10. nauseated
11. atrophy
12. opiates
13. malaise
14. panacea
15. contagious
16. quarantined
17. recuperate

Review Exercise–2 (Page 185)

CROSSWORD

ACROSS

1. phobic
2. opiate
3. atrophy
4. nausea
5. emollient
6. malaise
7. myopic

DOWN

1. panacea
2. infirmity
3. contagious
4. placebo
5. endemic
6. pestilence

CHAPTER 15

Practice Exercise (Page 195)

1. complete, whole
2. take forcibly
3. create mystery
4. old and ineffective
5. without luxury
6. rebellion
7. withdrawing
8. descendent
9. mysterious
10. looking at past
11. whole
12. new product
13. results
14. nobility
15. modern
16. ancestor
17. uncouth
18. latest
19. remember
20. unrecorded history
21. proletariat
22. new inventions
23. ancient
24. forgotten history
25. moments

Review Exercise–1 (Page 196)

2. A
3. B
4. B
5. E
6. E
7. B
8. D
9. C
10. A
11. D
12. A
13. B
14. A
15. B
16. A
17. C
18. D

Review Exercise–2 (Page 198)

1. remnants
2. mausoleums
3. spartan
4. scion
5. commemorate
6. superannuated
7. chronicled
8. vestiges
9. annals
10. obsolescence
11. unravel
12. usurp
13. retrospective
14. antediluvian
15. aeons

CHAPTER 16

Practice Exercise (Page 209)

1. foolish
2. think deeply
3. wise, careful
4. leave undone
5. proposal
6. of dull brain
7. fore-knowledge
8. early bird
9. read carefully
10. clearly expressed
11. confused
12. lacking foresight
13. thoughtful
14. an inspiring personality
15. intellectual class
16. understand
17. unknowledgeable
18. based on observation
19. explain
20. free thinker
21. judgement
22. understandable
23. amateur
24. not think
25. expert
26. knowledge
27. act hastily
28. powerful
29. brainless
30. shrewd
31. determine
32. create dispute
33. inform
34. not decide
35. settle matter
36. mental dullness
37. sharpness

Review Exercise–1 (Page 211)

1. empirical
2. sagacity
3. ruminate
4. cogitating
5. cogent
6. ascertain
7. prudence
8. apprised
9. unfathomable
10. discernible
11. cerebral
12. perspicacity
13. acumen
14. discretion
15. astute
16. proposition
17. precognition
18. pensive
19. luminaries
20. prodigy
21. precocious
22. erudition
23. propounded
24. elucidate
25. contemplate
26. cognizance
27. appraisal
28. acuity

Review Exercise–2 (Page 213)

A (i). B
(ii). D
(iii). C
(iv). D

B

(i) acumen
(ii) cogent
(iii) cerebral
(iv) connoisseur
(v) dilettante
(vi) emeritus
(vii) luminary
(viii) intelligentsia
(ix) pensive
(x) perspicuous
(xi) perceptive
(xii) precognition
(xiii) adjudicate
(xiv) arbitrate
(xv) propound
(xvi) apprise
(xvii) appraisal
(xviii) ruminate
(xix) laureate
(xx) proctor

CHAPTER 17

Practice Exercise (Page 226)

1. B
2. A
3. B
4. D
5. E
6. B
7. D
8. A
9. A
10. B
11. A
12. E
13. A
14. D
15. B
16. D
17. A
18. B
19. A
20. E

Review Exercise–1 (Page 228)

1. (v)
2. (x)
3. (k)
4. (t)
5. (u)
6. (e)
7. (w)
8. (p)
9. (z)
10. (c^1)
11. (d^1)
12. (b)
13. (f^1)
14. (l)
15. (d)
16. (y)
17. (c)
18. (j)
19. (j^1)
20. (s)
21. (m)
22. (h)
23. (b^1)
24. (e^1)
25. (o)
26. (g^1)
27. (h^1)
28. (g)
29. (i^1)
30. (r)
31. (q)
32. (a^1)
33. (i)
34. (n)
35. (f)
36. (a)
37. (k^1)
38. (l^1)

Review Exercise–2 (Page 229)

1. soliloquies
2. addendum
3. allusions
4. apropos
5. anthology
6. archaic
7. catharsis
8. clichèd
9. herculean
10. pseudonym
11. pastoral
12. plagiarism
13. genres
14. sublimity
15. allegory
16. corollary
17. protege
18. pathos
19. analogies
20. hyperbole

CHAPTER 18

Practice Exercise (Page 239)

1. disloyal to partner
2. disinclination
3. flexible
4. remain away
5. repulsion
6. feeling of desire
7. friendly
8. enmity
9. loyalty
10. displease
11. feeling of love
12. repelled
13. lifeless
14. trustworthy
15. agreement
16. distrust
17. friendly atmosphere
18. disgusted
19. feeling of love
20. animosity
21. friendly
22. unpleasant
23. rigid
24. liking
25. association
26. social

Review Exercise–1 (Page 240)

1. (c)	4. (b)	7. (f)	10. (i)	13. (w)	16. (n)	19. (p)	22. (r)	25. (y)
2. (a)	5. (h)	8. (e)	11. (m)	14. (x)	17. (l)	20. (q)	23. (s)	
3. (k)	6. (g)	9. (j)	12. (d)	15. (u)	18. (o)	21. (v)	24. (t)	

Review Exercise–2 (Page 241)

1. bewitching
2. camaraderie
3. liaisons
4. infatuation
5. compliant
6. proclivity
7. affability
8. endearing
9. geniality
10. enamoured
11. fraternity
12. enraptured
13. inclination
14. amenable
15. amicable
16. concord
17. convivial
18. affiliations

CHAPTER 19

Practice Exercise (Page 249)

1. lend without interest
2. spend excessively
3. expand
4. careful
5. sensible about money
6. net salary
7. riches
8. not related with money
9. inherited from male ancestor
10. thrifty
11. not related with money
12. related to trade
13. profitable
14. not give any surety
15. decrement
16. poor
17. tip
18. free
19. extravagant
20. take honestly
21. excessive
22. increase
23. refuse to share the cost
24. decrease
25. multiply

Review Exercise–1 (Page 250)

1. escalating
2. penury
3. pecuniary
4. squandering
5. perquisites
6. prodigal
7. retrenched
8. lucrative
9. augment
10. filching
11. frugality
12. indemnity
13. exorbitant
14. accrued
15. gratis
16. gratuity
17. parsimonious
18. mercantile
19. mercenary
20. impecunious
21. defray
22. usury

CROSSWORD (Page 252)

ACROSS

1. filching
2. escalate
3. gratuity
4. mercenary
5. penury
6. squander
7. gratis
8. pecuniary

DOWN

1. lucrative
2. augment
3. retrench
4. increment
5. patrimony
6. accrue

CHAPTER 20

Practice Exercise (Page 266)

1. dispute
2. polite
3. slander
4. done for another
5. revenge
6. appreciate
7. pleasure
8. having fear
9. false
10. divide
11. simple and straight
12. unprincipled person
13. not worth liking
14. resentful
15. calm and sweet
16. normal behavior
17. uplifting
18. include in society
19. normal
20. abusive
21. indifferent
22. rude
23. thankless
24. contort
25. under control
26. understated
27. create good feeling
28. irritate
29. worsen
30. motivate
31. criticism
32. enthusiastic
33. hateful
34. disgusting
35. harmful
36. sugar-coated
37. diplomatic
38. horrifying
39. bitterness
40. sweet

Review Exercise–1 (Page 267)

1. acrimonious
2. contention
3. brusqueness
4. vicarious
5. vendetta
6. vituperative
7. wrangling
8. caustic
9. deleterious
10. exacerbated
11. execrate
12. despicable
13. disparaging
14. diatribe
15. fractious
16. exasperated
17. insolence
18. insouciant
19. grimace
20. morbid
21. ostracism
22. perverted
23. pejorative
24. flagrantly
25. rancorous
26. promiscuous
27. pugnacious
28. irascibility
29. reprehensible
30. schism

Review Exercise–2 (a) (Page 269)

1. acerbic
2. vituperative
3. reprehensible
4. morbid
5. contentious
6. rancorous

Review Exercise–2 (b) (Page 270)

1. contumacious
2. petulent
3. vilify
4. trepidation
5. specious
6. umbrage
7. vendetta
8. upbraid
9. vicarious
10. wrangle

CHAPTER 21

Practice Exercise (Page 282)

1. very careful
2. honesty
3. approval
4. fondness
5. perfect
6. typical example
7. criticism
8. make less
9. song of praise
10. trivialise
11. praising
12. diatribe
13. ordinary
14. condemn
15. common place
16. invective
17. support
18. unworthy
19. centre of attraction
20. incomplete
21. provoking
22. pleasing
23. criticism
24. mercy
25. coax
26. prove genuine
27. favourable
28. noble
29. reduce
30. war
31. approval
32. ruffle
33. self-confidence
34. lessen
35. selfless
36. reduction
37. opposing
38. criticism
39. nadir
40. awards
41. humiliation

Review Exercise–1 (Page 284)

1. espousing
2. exemplary
3. cynosure
4. paeans
5. probity
6. approbation
7. armistice
8. complaisant
9. plaudits
10. impeccable
11. conciliation
12. extolling
13. panegyrics
14. lionized
15. kudos
16. appease
17. punctilious
18. paradigm
19. advocacy
20. commendation
21. august
22. palliative

Review Exercise–2 (Page 285)

1. F
2. D
3. G
4. E
5. C
6. A
7. B

CHAPTER 22

Practice Exercise (Page 293)

1. (k)
2. (o)
3. (r)
4. (i)
5. (a)
6. (j)
7. (v)
8. (d)
9. (b)
10. (c)
11. (a[1])
12. (x)
13. (t)
14. (e)
15. (z)
16. (s)
17. (f)
18. (y)
19. (w)
20. (u)
21. (p)
22. (q)
23. (n)
24. (m)
25. (l)
26. (g)
27. (h)

Review Exercise–1 (Page 294)

1. fulcrum
2. funicular
3. projectile
4. translucent
5. propellant
6. nautical
7. levitating
8. embryonic
9. incubate
10. hallucination
11. galvanized
12. alchemy
13. fuselage
14. matrix
15. momentum
16. fumigate
17. geneology
18. torque
19. fermenting
20. volatile

Review Exercise–2 (Page 295)

2. S
3. N
4. A
5. S
6. A
7. A
8. S
9. N
10. A
11. N
12. S
13. A
14. S
15. S

CHAPTER 23

Practice Exercise (Page 304)

1. profundity
2. strong
3. fuzzy
4. escalate
5. broad framed
6. short-sighted
7. unlimited
8. small details
9. big
10. leader
11. miniature
12. sufficient
13. enough
14. large
15. little
16. unimportant
17. huge
18. strengthen
19. small
20. tiny
21. reduction
22. restrict
23. in detail
24. collection
25. expansion
26. decrease
27. reduce
28. shortening

Review Exercise–1 (Page 305)

1. paltry
2. inconsequential
3. conciseness
4. abridging/brevity
5. diminutive
6. compendium
7. exiguous
8. minuscule
9. petite
10. myopic
11. modicum
12. succinctly
13. trivial
14. microcosm
15. minutiae
16. lilliputian
17. measly
18. dwarfish
19. infinitesimal
20. minions
21. enervated
22. meagre

Review Exercise–2 (Page 307)

2. N
3. S
4. S
5. N
6. S
7. S
8. A
9. N
10. S
11. A
12. N
13. N
14. S
15. S
16. N
17. N
18. S
19. N
20. N
21. N
22. A
23. A
24. N

CHAPTER 24

Practice Exercise (Page 315)

1. afflictions
2. morose
3. desolate
4. languished
5. dispirited
6. dolorous
7. aggrieved
8. penitent
9. bereavement
10. despondency
11. disconsolately
12. lamented
13. dolorous
14. maudlin
15. crestfallen
16. plaintive
17. contrite
18. sombre
19. woefully
20. scourge
21. rueing
22. tribulations

Review Exercise–1 (Page 317)

2. desolate
3. contrition
4. dispirited
5. despondent
6. languish
7. dolorous
8. paranoia
9. woeful
10. sombre
11. solemnity
12. scourge
13. plaintive
14. bereaved
15. tribulation
16. rueful

Review Exercise–2 (Page 318)

1. crestfallen
2. dispirited
3. penitent
4. disconsolate
5. morose
6. maudlin
7. desolate
8. despondent
9. excruciating
10. scourge

CHAPTER 25

Practice Exercise (Page 327)

1. modest
2. falter
3. having a complex
4. improper
5. made-up
6. unassuming
7. vain
8. showing ignorance
9. treat with superiority
10. obsequious
11. not patriotic
12. disrespectful
13. rude
14. suppliant
15. lack of confidence
16. humble
17. oppressed
18. look up to
19. authoritarian
20. appreciative
21. uplifting
22. proud
23. smugness
24. pleasure
25. polite
26. excessive pride
27. artificiality

Review Exercise–1 (Page 328)

1. domineering
2. pompous
3. chagrin
4. conceited
5. audacious
6. complacency
7. contemptuous
8. arrogance
9. swagger/haughtiness
10. impertinent
11. hubris/patronising
12. officious
13. affectation
14. vainglorious
15. imperious
16. condescending
17. supercilious
18. jingoism

Review Exercise–2 (Page 330)

CROSSWORD

ACROSS

1. despotic
2. jingoism
3. audacious
4. haughty
5. arrogance
6. swagger
7. conceited

DOWN

1. domineering
2. pompous
3. disdainful
4. hubris
5. patronise
6. complacency
7. insolent
8. affectations
9. chagrin
10. imperious

CHAPTER 26

Practice Exercise (Page 341)

2. rampage
3. lambast
4. apocalypse
5. bludgeon
6. brandish
7. pillage
8. fracas
9. fulminate
10. holocaust
11. cataclysm
12. blitzkrieg
13. annihilation
14. detonation
15. conflagration
16. carnage
17. onslaught
18. brawl
19. catapult
20. turbulence
21. imbroglio
22. paroxysm
23. foment
24. disarmament
25. catastrophe
26. mutinous
27. incarcerate
28. incendiary

Review Exercise–1 (Page 342)

1. detonate
2. conflagration
3. pillage
4. maelstrom
5. turbulence
6. disarmament
7. fomenting
8. skirmishes
9. fracas
10. rampage
11. catapult
12. holocaust
13. paroxysm
14. brandished
15. bombarded
16. blistering
17. truculent
18. annihilation
19. blitzkrieg
20. mutinous

Review Exercise–2 (Page 344)

1. A
2. S
3. N
4. S
5. S
6. A
7. S
8. S
9. A
10. S
11. A
12. S
13. S
14. N
15. S
16. S
17. A
18. A